CompuServe Almanac

An Offline Reference of Online Services

Third Edition

Disclaimer

This publication introduces the CompuServe Information Service and briefly describes many of the available services and products. The almanac does not purport to provide a comprehensive catalogue of CompuServe offerings, nor to present detailed explanations or instructions regarding those which are discussed. Furthermore, CompuServe Incorporated reserves the right to modify or eliminate any of its online services and products at any time, with or without published notification.

Trademarks

PREFACE

Welcome:

This Almanac contains concise descriptions of hundreds of helpful products and services available through the CompuServe Information Service. As North America's number one information service, CompuServe helps you make the best use of your personal computer.

Browse through the descriptions contained in the Almanac and you will quickly see that CompuServe has something for everyone.

If you are already a CompuServe subscriber, then the Almanac is a valuable guide to services that are at your fingertips. If you are not yet a CompuServe subscriber, the Almanac is an excellent introduction to what CompuServe offers.

To subscribe to CompuServe, all you need is a personal computer or terminal, a modem, communication software and a CompuServe Subscription Kit. CompuServe Subscription Kits are sold at computer and consumer retail outlets nationwide.

The Almanac is organized in chapters that reflect the 12 choices on the top menu. Within each chapter the products are arranged the way you would encounter them if you would branch through CompuServe's menu structure picking the first choice on the first menu, then the first choice on that menu and so on until you covered every menu choice. The service constantly grows and changes so that even as this manual was being printed, new products were being added. You will find new services, the removal of some old ones and some readjustment of the menu structure. For this reason we have provided you with the quick reference word or a page number used to locate products on the CompuServe Information Service. We have also provided room for you to write in the Almanac so that you can write down helpful tips or the addresses of your friends on the service, and page numbers within products that pinpoint your interests.

Some services appear on more than one menu so they appear in the corresponding places in the Almanac. The one exception is the Electronic Mall which is described in its entirety (at the time of publication) only in Chapter 6 — The Electronic Mall/Shopping.

This Almanac does not replace any other CompuServe publication. You will need to consult the CompuServe Users Guide for detailed information on using the service.

We have included a few command summaries in Appendix A for your convenience. Also included in the Appendix are time zones, state codes, popular stock market codes and other useful information.

Use your Almanac and enjoy exploring the CompuServe Information Service. We think you will be amazed at all you will find and the many ways you can use the service for your personal and professional benefit.

Enjoy.

CompuServe

The Almanac is designed to acquaint you with the different products on the CompuServe Information Service. If you are already a CompuServe subscriber, you probably have discovered certain areas in the Service that you know and enjoy. Perhaps you already check stock information (GO MQUOTE), chat on CB (GO CB), or are a member of one or more forums. But there are other areas that could also benefit you. For example, if you plan a vacation or a business trip, you can check airline prices, schedules and availability, and then book your flight using one or more of the products in the travel section. You can use the Service to swap condo time or rent an RV. If someone in your family has a medical condition, you can do some quick research or question an expert (GO HNT). Or you can shop and bank using your keyboard (GO SHOPPING) (GO BANKING).

The choices available on CompuServe are called products, and each is created and maintained by a different sponsor. Therefore each product is a little different and may require its own set of commands. But there are certain things that are always true no matter which product you are using.

1. You can return to the top menu by entering T at any ! prompt. You may, however, need to exit certain parts of a product before you can get to a ! prompt to return to the top menu.

2. You can always get a list of available commands by entering ? at any prompt.

3. Products that have a surcharge are indicated by a $ on their menu choice and following their product description in the Almanac. Therefore, it is difficult to incur a surcharge accidentally. The Almanac shows a $* if part of the product has a surcharge. An **E** means the product is part of the Executive Option.

4. Consult your CompuServe Information Service Users Guide. It contains assistance on how to use the service and instructions for certain products. The Users Guide can make your online use much faster and easier by giving you the tools you need to use the service. The Almanac shows you all the different exciting areas of the service.

How The Almanac Is Organized

The Almanac is organized the same way the menus are on theCompuServe Information Service. There are 12 chapters, one for each of the 12 choices on the Top or Main Menu.

Chapter 1 — Subscriber Assistance
Chapter 2 — Find a Topic
Chapter 3 — Communication/Bulletin Boards
Chapter 4 — News/Weather/Sports
Chapter 5 — Travel/Leisure
Chapter 6 — The Electronic Mall/Shopping
Chapter 7 — Money Matters/Markets
Chapter 8 — Entertainment/Games
Chapter 9 — Home/Health/Family
Chapter 10 — Reference/Education
Chapter 11 — Computers/Technology
Chapter 12 — Business/Other Interests.

Each chapter then follows in order of the menu choices and subchoices.

Suppose from the top menu you enter choice 9, HOME/ HEALTH/FAMILY. You then get a menu with eight choices from FOOD/WINE to REFERENCE MATERIAL. In the Almanac Chapter 9, HOME/HEALTH/FAMILY, has eight sections corresponding to the eight menu choices.

But again, the service is constantly changing so new productsmay appear that shift the old ones around a little, usually up or down one menu choice. Fortunately for navigation the top menu selection remains fairly stable and related products remain grouped together. As a pioneer in the new world of electronic communications, have fun and explore!

Typical Description

Each product description in the Almanac has a similar format:

Product Number   Product Name   Quick Reference Word

7.2.6
Disclosure II   **DISCLOSURE**
The Disclosure II database is compiled from the 10K reports that all publicly-owned companies file with the Securities and Exchange Commission. This information includes financial statements and ratios, business segment data, 5-year financial summaries, company name and address, a list of SEC filings, a business description, officers and directors, an ownership and subsidiary summary, and lists of insider owners, institutional owners, and owners of 5% or more of the company's stock. It also includes the management discussion. See Appendix F for a list of optionable stocks.
    Updated weekly with market prices updated daily. **$**E

Product Description   This product has   This product is
                                           a surcharge.   part of the
                                                                   Executive Option.

Product Numbers

When the Almanac was organized, each product had a number assigned based on the menu choices you would make to reach the product from the top menu. These product numbers are included for you. Here is an example of how you can use the product number 9.3.6 to go from the top menu to PaperChase:

9.3.6
PaperChase (MEDLINE)   **PCH**

Start at the top menu: (GO TOP or T[CR])

Press **9** for **Home/Health/Family**. From that menu

Press **3** for **Health/Fitness**. From that menu

Press **6** for **PaperChase**.

The numbers were correct at the time of printing but are subject to change. We suggest that if you choose to navigate using the product number, you replace old numbers with current numbers for your favorite products.

Plan Your Session

We suggest that you plan your sessions on CompuServe. Usethe Almanac to find the products you wish to use and list their Quick Reference Words or page numbers. As you navigate the service, you may find other products that also interest you. Either add them to your list or note them for your next session.

You may want to make it a habit to peek in on one or two new products each session. That way you will always be expanding your familiar territory.

CONTENTS

CONTENTS

CONTENTS

CONTENTS

CONTENTS

Product/Service	Quick Reference Word	Almanac Page Number
(Chapter 3 continued)		

CONTENTS

CONTENTS

CONTENTS

Product/Service	Quick Reference Word	Almanac Page Number
Chapter 5 — Travel/Leisure		

CONTENTS

Product/Service	Quick Reference Word	Almanac Page Number

CONTENTS

CONTENTS

CONTENTS

CONTENTS

CONTENTS

CONTENTS

Product/Service	Quick Reference Word	Almanac Page Number

CONTENTS

CONTENTS

CONTENTS

Product/Service	Quick Reference Word	Almanac Page Number

CONTENTS

CONTENTS

CONTENTS

CONTENTS

CONTENTS

CONTENTS

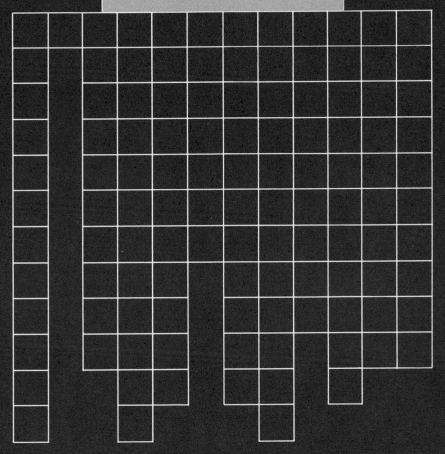

Subscriber Assistance 1
Find A Topic 2
Communications/Bulletin Boards 3
News/Weather/Sports 4
Travel and Leisure 5
The Electronic Mall/Shopping 6
Money Matters and Markets 7
Entertainment/Games 8
Home/Health/Family 9
Reference/Education 10
Computer and Technology 11
Business/Other Interests 12

This chapter helps you find your way around the CompuServe Information Service. It provides information on billing, logon, ordering, operating rules and more.

1

1.1.1
Tour   **TOUR**
The CompuServe Guided Tour takes you on a quick trip through the Service giving you an overview of what's available in each of the top menu categories. After each section you have the option of continuing on the Tour or learning more about that section.

1.1.2
Find a Topic   **INDEX**
CompuServe indexes products by topic and alphabetically. In INDEX, if you enter a topic such as food or sports, you are given a menu list of CompuServe products and their Quick Reference Words or page numbers. Enter the GO command with either the Quick Reference Word or page number to quickly go to the product. You can also get an alphabetical listing of all CompuServe products and their Quick Reference Words.

Actually, if you are at any ! prompt in the CompuServe Information Service, the index is available by entering the FIND command.

1.2
Online Today Electronic Edition   **OLT**
The Electronic Edition of CompuServe's *Online Today* magazine. The *Online Today Electronic Edition* provides daily updated computer and information industry news, CompuServe news, product announcements, reviews of new hardware, software, books and more.

1.2.7
Online Today Online Inquiry   **OLI**
You can request general information about an ad displayed in *Online Today* and request product literature directly from advertisers.

1.3
Command Summary/How To Use   **COMMAND**
This menu choice explains the commands that can be used in the CompuServe Information Service and how to use them. It explains how the menus work, control characters, and communication standards. It also lists access telephone numbers and gives access to billing information.

1.3.6.1
Telephone Access Numbers   **PHONES**
This menu lists network access telephone numbers that connect to the CompuServe Information Service.

1.3.6.2
International Access Numbers   **CSCNET**
This menu lists international access telephone numbers that connect to the CompuServe Information Service.

1.3.6.3
Node Abbreviations   **NODES**
This menu lists the unique three-letter CompuServe codes which indicate a subscriber's local telephone access point.

1.3.7
Billing Information   **BILLING**
Refer to 1.8

1.3.8
Current Rates   **RATES**
This section lists the fees associated with CompuServe's use and the billing options available to subscribers.

1.3.9
Quick Reference Words   **QUICK**
A list of Quick Reference Words is provided. The Quick Reference Words are used following the GO command to quickly take you to the product named. In the Almanac Quick Reference Words are at the upper right corner of each description. Example: GO QUICK

1.4
What's New This Week   **NEW**
This menu shows you what is new on the service this week. It includes news from the Electronic Mall, Forum conference schedules, CompuServe community news and the *Online Today Magazine Electronic Edition*. You can either choose a topic or enter a carriage return to go to the top menu.

1.5
Logon/Logoff Instructions   **LOGON**

Instructions are available for logging on using the CompuServe, TYMNET, Telenet, DataPac, LATA and Computer Sciences Corporation communications networks. You can locate access phone numbers using location, baud rate or local telephone exchange matching. You will also find help in logging off without generating additional charges, information on network problems, and node abbreviations and their geographic locations.

1.6
Ask Customer Service   **QUESTION**

Customer Service makes it easy to get the help you need whenever you need it.

When a question comes up while you're online, type GO QUESTION to visit the Questions and Answers service. Customer Service provides a list of commonly asked questions about CompuServe and their answers. Questions are answered on such topics as EasyPlex, billing, forums, logon, CB and VIDTEX. Customer Service is continually updating the Questions and Answers database to keep up with the growing Information Service.

When you can't find the assistance you need in users guides or online, let Customer Service answer your individual questions. Customer Service representatives help subscribers solve any problems they may encounter and encourage their comments. Type GO FEEDBACK to visit the Feedback area to send questions, comments or suggestions to CompuServe.

If you have a question or problem that requires immediate attention, such as logging on, a Customer Service Representative can help you. Subscribers within Ohio and from outside the U.S. can call (614) 457-8650. Subscribers from outside Ohio and within the U.S. including Hawaii, Alaska, Puerto Rico, St. Thomas, St. John and St. Croix can call (800) 848-8990. Representatives are generally available from 8 A.M. to midnight, Monday through Friday and from 2 P.M. to midnight on weekends, Eastern Time. Holiday hours vary.

1.6.2
Feedback to CompuServe   **FEEDBACK**

Feedback enables you to send your question, comment or suggestion to CompuServe. Your connect time is free while you are in FEEDBACK, although you will still be charged for any communication surcharges. You'll be told upon exiting FEEDBACK when connect charges resume.

The Customer Service Representative will answer via EasyPlex as quickly as possible.

1.7
Change Your User Profile   **PROFILE**
This menu choice enables you to change the way that information is displayed on
your screen or printer. You can also change your password or billing option and notify
CompuServe of your change of address. More information on these areas can be found in
the *Users Guide*.

1.7.1
Terminal Settings   **TERMINAL**
                                                   OPTIONS

This powerful area enables you to change your terminal type, your settings such as line
length, baud rate, parity, and printer delay, as well as your first logon action. In addition,
you can build your own personal menu of products that will display at logon.

1.7.2
Change Your Password   **PASSWORD**
This menu choice enables you to change your password.

1.7.4
Change Your Billing Options   **BILOPT**
You can change your billing option from CHECKFREE to credit card or from one credit
card to another. If your card has been recently renewed and you need to enter the new
expiration date, you can use this option to do so.

1.7.5
Change Your Billing Address   **ADDRESS**
Use this choice to change your billing address.

1.8
Billing Information   **BILLING**
View your charges or look up current rates in this service area. You will find explanations
of the available billing options and general billing information that is helpful for you to
know. You can also change your billing option, change your billing address or select the
Executive Option.

1.8.1
Current Rates   **RATES**
Refer to 1.3.8

1.8.2
Reviewing Your Charges/Usage   **CHARGES**

Review your usage and your charges as current as yesterday's log off and typically as far back as eight weeks. See for yourself when your payment is posted, which services you used that generated a surcharge, credits applied and your account balance. You can also find explanations of each billing option's billing period.

1.8.3
Billing Options Explained   **BIL-33**

This section explains the various billing options available to CompuServe subscribers including VISA, MasterCard, American Express, CHECKFREE and Business Account.

1.8.4
Change Your Billing Address   **ADDRESS**

Use this choice to change your billing address.

1.8.5
Change Your Billing Option   **BILOPT**

Refer to 1.7.4

1.8.6
Order Executive Option   **EXECUTIVE**

CompuServe's Executive Service Option enables you to access additional value-added services, purchase many CompuServe products at a discount, and increase your online storage capabilities, including increasing the storage period from 30 days to six months.

Online services offered through the Executive Option are marked with an (E) on menus. These products currently include:

Financial products	— Ticker Retrieval
	Security Screening
	Return Analysis
	DISCLOSURE II
	Institutional Brokers Estimate System
	Company Screening
News	— Executive News Service (ENS)
Demographics	— Supersite

Executive subscribers also receive direct marketing offers from many of CompuServe's affiliated merchants and manufacturers.

Most executive products display best on 80 column screens.

1.8.7

General Billing Information   **BILINF**

This section provides detailed information on your bill and ways to inquire about questionable bills. It tells you how to submit error correction requests to CompuServe. It also tells you how to avoid unauthorized use of your account and what to do if you suspect unauthorized use.

1.9

Order from CompuServe   **ORDER**

Access CompuServe's online ordering service and place your order selecting from CompuServe's many exciting products — from users guides, T-shirts, game maps, posters and more. You can also check on an existing order's status and change an order before it is filled. You are not charged for connect time viewing descriptions or placing an order. You are, however, charged for communications surcharges.

1.10.1

CompuServe Information Service Operating Rules   **RULES**

This section offers a complete description of the CompuServe Operating Rules. The Operating Rules are designed to protect the data and communications offered by CompuServe information providers and customers and make online usage a positive experience for everyone.

1.10.2

Copyright/Ownership   **CPY**

Material offered on the service originates with a wide variety of sources. This section addresses commonly-asked questions about copyright and ownership of material particularly as it related to public domain information and shareware programs.

1.11

Subscriber Directory   **DIRECTORY**

The CompuServe Subscriber Directory enables you to search for other subscribers by name. All subscribers are included in the Subscriber Directory, unless they specifically request exclusion. Now you can obtain the User ID number of other subscribers and easily communicate with them via EasyPlex or through our other online communication services.

Find a
Topic   2

This chapter enables you to access CompuServe's product index. CompuServe indexes products by topic and alphabetically. In INDEX, if you enter a topic such as food or sports, you are given a menu list of CompuServe products and their Quick Reference Words or page numbers. Enter the GO command with either the Quick Reference Word or page number to quickly go to the product. You can also get an alphabetical listing of all CompuServe products and their Quick Reference Words.

Actually, if you are at any ! prompt in the CompuServe Information Service, the index is available by entering the FIND command.

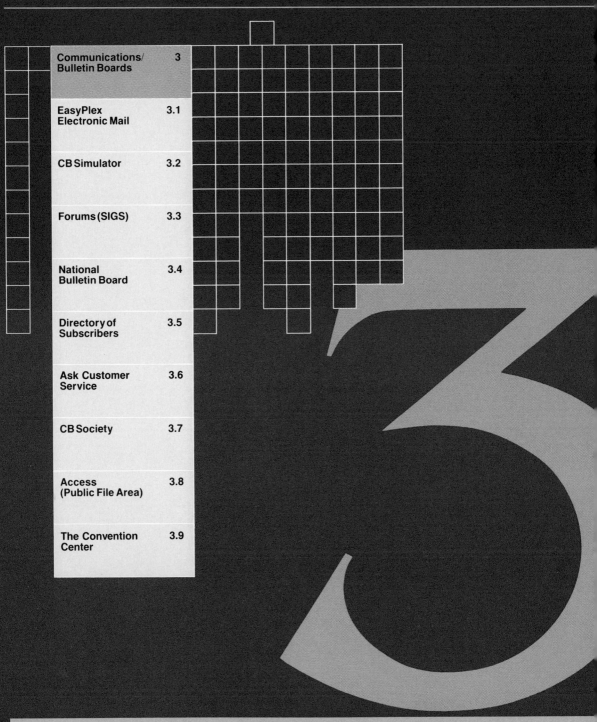

This chapter contains products that enable you to communicate with other CompuServe subscribers. You can use EasyPlex to send messages to specific people, forums to participate in discussions on specific topics, CB to party, and the National Bulletin Board to post bulletins. However you choose to communicate, the opportunities are there for you to make new friends and exchange ideas.

3.1
EasyPlex Electronic Mail   **EASY**

EasyPlex is CompuServe's electronic mail service. It gives you the opportunity to communicate not only with any EasyPlex user, but also with most InfoPlex (CompuServe's business electronic mail system) users, all MCI Mail subscribers and any TELEX machine in the world.

Using EasyPlex, you have the ability to upload and download messages from your personal computer, and file them in your PER Area. If you send a "receipt requested" message, you will find a notification in your mailbox when the message has been read by the recipient. There are three modes of operation in EasyPlex: MENU for novice users, PROMPT for intermediate users and COMMAND for expert users. There is also help available at most EasyPlex prompts. You have your choice of two editors when you compose your messages: a line-numbered editor and a nonline numbered editor.

EasyPlex has an electronic address book to store the names and user IDs of the people to whom you send messages. The Almanac also has an address book which is located in the Appendix.

There is a surcharge for sending "receipt requested" messages and for sending messages to InfoPlex users, MCI Mail subscribers and TELEX machines. **$***

3

3.2
CB Simulator   CB

CompuServe's CB Simulator is an electronic conferencing program. It's a little like CB radio, except that you use a computer or terminal and, instead of speaking into a microphone, you type at a keyboard. Your reach isn't limited to a few miles, either. You can converse with other people from all over the country, and even overseas.

3.2.2
CB Band A   CB-1

There are two bands of CB, each with 36 channels. You can access either through the Communications menu or by using the GO command.

3.2.3
CB Band B   CB-2

3.2.4
CB Club   CBCLUB

Special pricing is available for subscribers who use CB frequently.

3.2.5
CB Society — Cupcake's Column   CUPCAKE

Cupcake is our resident CB columnist. Here's where you can get the scoop on the latest party, who's engaged, who's new and what's happening.

3.2.6
CBIG Special Interest Forum   CBIG

CBIG is the Special Interest Group for CBers. CBIG consists of a bulletin board and member and data libraries. There are sections for CB personal ads, technology, handles, etc., as well as several valuable programs for split screen CBing and viewing CBers' digitized pictures.

3.2.7
CB Pictures   CBPIX

Scores of CBers have had their likenesses digitized for your viewing pleasure. If you have a computer with high-resolution graphics capability (RLE) and a software package that can translate the data, you can view these pictures. You can obtain additional online information about VIDTEX, CompuServe's telecommunications software (GO VIDTEX), and RLE graphics (GO PICS).

3.2.8
Nodes   CB-236
The nodes listing translates all the CompuServe acronyms for subscribers' points of connection into their respective cities and states. CBers can use the nodes listing to tell what CompuServe node other CBers are using. Supplemental network nodes are not included.

3.3
Forums (SIGs)   FORUMS
Forums are places where people of similar interests can exchange information, participate in discussions in real-time conferences or share software programs. There are three types of forums:

- Computer forums where you will find experts to solve problems or exchange technical ideas about computers
- Professional forums geared to specific professions like medicine or law, and
- General interest forums where people with similar interests exchange ideas or just have a good time.

All forums have a similar structure and use the same commands. They are run by one or more Forum Administrators (SysOps — system operators) who are in charge of the forum and have some expertise in the subject matter of the forum.

Most forums prefer that you use your full name, and they do not tolerate disruptive behavior.

There are three main areas of a forum:

- A message board containing hundreds of messages placed there by subscribers.
- A data library containing text files and programs that contain software, transcripts of conferences and essays.
- A conference mode where members get together for real-time conferences. This is similar to the CB Simulator.

For more information on forums and how to use forum commands, see the Users Guide.

3.3.1
Aviation Forums   COM-11
These forums are for people interested in aviation.

3.3.1.1
Aviation Forum   AVSIG
The Aviation Special Interest Forum is a group of people interested in computers and airplanes. It covers general flying issues, safety, weather, air traffic control, balloons and soaring, want ads and personal computer programs. AVSIG is open to any and all who care to visit and share their ideas and experience in the field of aviation.

3.3.1.2
ModelNet   **MODELNET**

The Model Aviation Forum is a forum for the model hobbyist. Builders of model railroads, airplanes, cars and boats will find all these disciplines covered in the forum. In addition, forum members have access to newsletters and articles from "Model Aviation Magazine" and a complete contest calendar. A "Swap Shop" enables hobbyists to trade parts.

3.3.2
Educational Forums   **EDU-50**

This section contains educational forums dealing with educational topics including disabilities, foreign language, science and math.

3.3.2.1
ADCIS Forum   **ADCIS**

The Association for the Development of Computer-Based Instructional Systems is a nonprofit association dedicated to advancing the investigation and utilization of computer-based education and training. Nonmembers of the organization can review information included in this forum.

3.3.2.2
Disabilities Forum   DISABILITIES

The Disabilities Forum is a communication facility for anyone interested in disabilities to exchange information. Disabled people share information, ideas and experiences related to their daily living. Parents and families of disabled people and professionals who work with disabled people also share their experiences and information.

The Disabilities Forum is open to eeveryone.

3.3.2.3
Computer Training Forum   DPTRAIN

The Computer Training Forum is for computer trainers, teachers, information center staff, vendors and anyone else with an opinion on the computer learning process. Data libraries contain information on training techniques, office automation, careers and computers in schools. International members contribute reports on computer trends overseas. Members can enroll in free online Professional Seminars taught by leading instructors across the country.

3.3.2.4
EPIE Forum   EPIEFORUM

The EPIE Forum is dedicated to the exchange of information and ideas concerning educational courseware, products and services. News and events of interest to computer-oriented educators, students and parents are discussed. The EPIE Forum is open to everyone.

A closely related product, the EPIE Database (GO EPE), has information on educational software and hardware.

3.3.2.5
Education Forum   EDFORUM

The Education Forum is designed to meet the diverse needs of people involved in the teaching and learning process. This includes teachers, parents, students, faculty members and other professionals in the education field. The increasing use of microcomputers and other high technologies in our schools and homes has been a natural topic of focus of discussion in this forum.

3.3.2.6
Educational Research Forum   EDRESEARCH

The Education Research Forum is for people who are interested in research about the process and products of education. Through the forum, the latest research findings are shared and compared, and a dialogue is established between researchers and educators in the schools. Sponsored by the Midwestern Educational Research Association.

3.3.2.7
Foreign Language Education Forum   **FLEFO**
The Foreign Language Forum provides a service to both general and specific interests in the area of foreign languages and foreign language learning. It includes:

- Conferences
- A job bank for translators, educators and students
- Information on legislation and factors influencing the foreign language profession and
- A list of professional organizations.

3.3.2.8
LOGO Forum   **LOGOFORUM**
The Logo Forum uses a light-hearted approach to explore the use of the Logo computer language and technologies that influence our lives. Cartoon characters keep interest high.

3.3.2.9
Science/Math Education Forum   **SCIENCE**
This forum serves a variety of needs for Science Educators, students and others with interests in science and science education. It includes a large data library of software which can be downloaded into class and home computers.

3.3.2.10
Students' Forum   **STUFO**
The Student's Forum is popular with middle school students who can share their ideas and interests with other students around the country. Teachers of junior high students exchange ideas on using the forum.

3.3.2.11
Space Education Forum   **SPACEED**
Teachers, motivated students, and anyone interested in the development of space-related curriculums in the classroom can exchange resources and ideas in the Space Education Forum. The agenda coincides with the Teacher in Space Education Foundation, directed by NASA's Teacher in Space Program. Members can discuss topics such as the use of innovative technology in the classroom and the direction for future education in the U.S.

3.3.2.12
AEJMC Forum   **AEJMC**

The AEJMC Forum is a good source of information for journalism professionals, teachers, researchers, and students. This forum is sponsored by the Association for Education in Journalism and Mass Communication. In it journalists discuss ethics and share tips for researching stories, job opening information, and ideas for covering stories.

3.3.3
Science/Technology Forums   **PCS-40**

These forums are for people interested in ham radio, space, electronics, and science fiction.

3.3.3.1
Astronomy Forum   **ASTROFORUM**

Amateur or professional stargazers can join cosmic forces with fellow astronomers from around the world. Beginners with a universe of questions can learn about hardware or techniques. Professionals can take advantage of the Astronomy Forum to rapidly disseminate information among colleges. Members of all levels can learn about national or international special events of interest. Archives contain public domain astronomy software and quality reference articles.

3.3.3.3
Computer Training Forum   **DPTRAIN**
Refer to 3.3.2.3

3.3.3.4
Consumer Electronics Forum   **CEFORUM**
The Consumer Electronics Forum is dedicated to exchanging information about electronic consumer products such as VCRs, telephone answering machines, compact disk players, and even earth station equipment. The forum features articles, reviews, new products and news in its data libraries. You can get answers for your questions and discuss the latest issues facing this industry. Special interactive online conferences feature guests from manufacturers such as Sony, Pioneer and Panasonic.

3.3.3.5
HamNet (Ham Radio) Online   **HAM**
HamNet Online is dedicated to serving the needs of amateur radio and short-wave listening (SWL) enthusiasts. You will find:

- Information on getting started in ham radio and SWL,
- The latest news and information on ham radio and SWL events,
- Regular "electronic editions" of amateur radio and SWL newsletters and
- Information on new technical developments.

3.3.3.5.3
HamNet (Ham Radio) Forum   **HAMNET**
This is the conferencing facility of HamNet Online and is where you can converse with others who are interested in amateur radio and short wave listening.

3.3.3.7
Photography Forum   **PHOTOFORUM**
Shutterbugs of all levels, professional and amateur, can meet in the Photography Forum. Members can discuss photography equipment, film types, and camera techniques. Professionals can communicate with others in the business and share money-making ideas.

3.3.3.8
Picture Support Forum   **PICS**

The Picture Support Forum is dedicated to expanding the availability of online graphics. This forum is for exchange of information on how to create and upload graphics files, to provide graphics files for those without the ability to create them, and to maintain a display area of graphics files for downloading. Members can share information about their techniques, tips, and traps.

3.3.3.9
Sci-Fi/Fantasy   **SCI**

Sci-Fi and Fantasy's forum serves the needs of people who are interested in science fiction and fantasy. You will find:

- The Science Fiction and Fantasy Forum (GO SCI-FI),
- The Comic Book Forum (GO COMIC),
- News about publishing, movie making, TV, conventions and
- Book reviews and commentaries.

3.3.3.9.1
Sci-Fi/Fantasy Forum   **SCI-FI**

The Sci-Fi Forum is a place where people who enjoy Science Fiction can get together and chat about their mutual likes and dislikes. There are also conferences with famous authors, producers and publishers.

3.3.3.9.2
Comic Book Forum   **COMIC**

This forum features news, reviews and conferences with some of the greats of comic books and animations.

3.3.3.10
Science/Math Education Forum   **SCIENCE**

Refer to 3.3.2.9

3.3.3.11
Space Education Forum   **SPACEED**

Refer to 3.3.2.11

3.3.3.12
Space Forum   **SPACEFORUM**

Space Forum is for subscribers interested in all aspects of space exploration, travel, research, colonization, research and development, and related activities. NASA news releases are posted regularly in this forum.

3.3.4
Entertainment/Games Forums   **EGFORUMS**

This section contains the forums for people who like to have fun by playing computer games.

3.3.4.1
CBIG (CB Interest Group)   **CBIG**
Refer to 3.2.6

3.3.4.2
Comic Book Forum   **COMIC**
Refer to 3.3.3.9.2

3.3.4.3
Consumer Electronics Forum   **CEFORUM**
Refer to 3.3.3.4

3

3.3.4.4
Gaming Connection   **GAMECON**
The Gaming Connection is your gateway to three forums: ELECTRONIC GAMER (GO EGAMER), the Gamers' Forum (GO GAMERS) and Multi-Player Games Forum (GO MPGAMES).

3.3.4.4.1
The ELECTRONIC GAMER™   **EGAMER**
The ELECTRONIC GAMER™ is an online magazine for all people who are interested in games. Updated twice monthly, TEG is staffed by editors who are expert gamers. Included in TEG are complete step-by-step "walkthrus" of popular computer games (such as the ZORK series by Infocom and the ULTIMA series by Lord British). A game hints section is available for players who want a nudge in the right direction rather than an explicit answer. New game reviews are continuously added to the magazine. "TFG's Gazette" is a magazine within a magazine and contains articles previously published in print magazines, commentary, humor, and fiction. If you're interested in games, The ELECTRONIC GAMER™ will inform and entertain you.

3.3.4.4.2
Gamers' Forum   **GAMERS**
It's a computer game player's dream: an electronic forum dedicated to the communication, support and entertainment needs of the CompuServe game-playing community.
    Activity conducted in this forum encompasses games conducted outside the CompuServe environment, games conducted via the Gamers' Forum conference area and message boards, and single-player games conducted within the CompuServe environment. If you have any questions or would like to discuss such games with other persons via a public forum, this is the place to do it.

3.3.4.4.3
Multi-Player Games Forum   MPGAMES

An online forum dedicated to the communication, support, and entertainment needs of people who play any of the multi-player games via CompuServe's online environment. As a result of their multi-player nature and the complexity of the games' content, the games are rather challenging.

Players who have questions about any of the multi-player games are encouraged to use the forum to get answers to those questions from other players and from the Games' Forum Administrators. The forum serves as an exchange of ideas and hints to help you play the games. It also provides players with a way to communicate with teammates to plan strategy and to conduct online conference meetings.

3.3.4.5
General Music Forum   MUSICFORUM

The Music Forum is a forum for discussing classical, jazz, popular, blues, country and western, rock and foreign music. There are weekly conferences. The database contains live interviews done in the Music Forum, a top-40 countdown, computer music programs and articles about music.

3.3.4.6
Picture Support Forum   PICS
Refer to 3.3.3.8

3.3.4.7
RockNet   ROCK

RockNet provides the music enthusiast with up-to-the-minute news and information on the world of rock. It contains:

- The RockNet Forum (GO ROCKNET),
- Rock news,
- A list of top record reviews and
- Articles about rock music.

3.3.4.7.5
RockNet Forum   ROCKNET

The RockNet Forum has many members that are within the record industry, and you may learn news items before they appear in newspapers.

3.3.4.8
Sci-Fi/Fantasy   **SCI**
Refer to 3.3.3.9

3.3.4.8.1
Sci-Fi/Fantasy Forum   **SCI-FI**
Refer to 3.3.3.9.1

3.3.4.8.2
Comic Book Forum   **COMIC**
Refer to 3.3.3.9.2

3.3.4.9
WitSIG   **WITSIG**
WitSIG is dedicated to humor and entertainment. It is a place where you can come to relax and have a laugh or two after visiting the more serious areas of CompuServe.

3.3.5
Financial Forums   **FINFORUM**
This section contains financial forums. The Financial Forums enable you to ask specific questions about financial matters such as the economy, or about technical matters such as running Lotus Symphony. You'll be asking professionals who know their subject matter well, and you will have a chance to trade ideas with others like yourself.

3.3.5.1
Investors Forum   INVFORUM
The Investor's Forum is an area on CompuServe where anyone interested in the financial world may discuss topics of interest. The forum is administered by Forum Administrators who are well-versed in financial terms and strategies. A regularly scheduled real-time conference allows members to speak together about a myriad of financial topics. While many members are brokers or bankers, all are welcome.

3.3.5.2
National Association of Investors Forum   NAIC
The goal of the National Association of Investors Forum is to educate long-term investors in how to find quality companies and buy stocks at good prices. Well-managed companies are identified from reported financial data and in-depth analysis. Members can share information on portfolio management, software, and favorite stocks.

3.3.5.3
Ask Mr. Fed Forum   ASKFED
The Ask Mr. Fed Forum enables you to ask relevant questions of economists who are in touch with the inner workings of government activities. $

3.3.5.4
Javelin Forum   JAVELIN
Javelin Software's business analysis and reporting system uses a more structured approach to model building than the traditional spreadsheet. The Javelin Forum helps you take full advantage of Javelin's capabilities. These capabilities include the ability to "look behind the numbers" to determine where a specific number comes from and view problems in several ways including worksheets, formulas, and presentation-quality graphs. Members of Javelin Software Corporation are online to answer your questions and provide technical support.

3.3.5.5
Lotus 1-2-3 User Forum   LOTUS123
Lotus Development Corporation established the 1-2-3 Users Forum as part of the World of Lotus, and it is maintained by Lotus staff members. The forum provides registered members with the ability to:

- Read and leave messages to other members and to Lotus Development Corporation
- Upload and download applications software from the public domain libraries
- Share interests with other 1-2-3 members and
- Participate in online conferences.

3.3.5.6
Lotus Graphics Products   **LOTUSGRAPHIC**

Users of Freelance, Freelance Plus, and Graphwriter can exchange ideas in the Lotus Graphics Products Forum. Members discuss graphic business communication such as charts, diagrams, word charts, freehand drawings, symbols, and maps. Data libraries contain public domain software and symbols. A catalog of member interests and specialties can put you in touch with compatible fellow members.

3.3.5.7
Lotus Jazz Forum   **LOTUSJAZZ**

The Jazz Development Forum is the third forum in the World of Lotus. Like the 1-2-3 Users Forum and the Symphony Users Forum, registered members can:

- Read and leave messages to other members and to the Lotus Development Corporation
- Upload and download applications software from the public domain data library
- Share interest with other 1-2-3 members and
- Participate in online conferencing.

3.3.5.8
Lotus Symphony User Forum   **SYMPHONY**

The Symphony Users Forum is similar to the 1-2-3 Users Forum except that the subject matter is geared to Lotus Symphony.

3.3.5.9
Monogram Software Forum   **MONOGRAM**

Users of Monogram's software products, including Dollars and Sense and Moneyline, can use this forum to exchange information and applications. The data libraries are managed by Monogram Software's technical support and analysis department. The libraries contain answers to commonly asked questions, as well as examples of stock transactions, billing applications, credit card management and payroll administration. Monogram compatibility with IBM, Apple, Macintosh and Atari is also discussed.

3.3.6
Hardware Forums   **HARDWARE**

Hardware Forums enable users of particular hardware to exchange ideas. Many forums include extensive data libraries, software programs and interaction with hardware manufacturers.

3.3.6.1
Apple Users Group   **MAUG**

There are five forums devoted to Apple computers: the Macintosh Users Forum (GO MACUS), the Macintosh Business Forum (GO MACBIZ), the Apple Developers Forum (GO APPDEV), the Apple II and III Forum (GO APPLE) and Apples OnLine (GO AOL).

3.3.6.1.1
Macintosh Users Forum   **MACUS**

The Macintosh Users Forum is dedicated to users of the Macintosh line of computers, as well as the Macintosh's predecessor, the Lisa. Here you can find excellent public domain programs, stimulating conversation through the messaging systems, and conferences with notable software authors and high-level Apple executives such as John Sculley, Jean-Louis Gassee and others.

3.3.6.1.2
Macintosh Business Forum   **MACBIZ**

The MAUG Macintosh Business Forum is for Macintosh users in the business world. A variety of subjects are discussed in this forum including productivity software, spreadsheets, databases, desktop publishing, networks and accounting.

3.3.6.1.3
Apple Developers Forum   **APPDEV**

The Apple Developers Forum is geared toward developers of software and hardware for Apple personal computers. Members can discuss tools like languages, debuggers, editors and linkers, as well as hardware enhancements. The newsletters and tech notes provide up-to-date items on Apple products. Non-developers are welcome to join and take advantage of the data libraries.

3

3.3.6.1.4
Maug™ Apple II and III Forum   **APPLE**

The MAUG™ Apple II and III Forum is devoted to people interested in the use of either of these computers. People from all over the world exchange hints and techniques, opinions on hardware and software, and viewpoints. The database area contains a wide selection of software for the Apple II and III computers. There are conferences with celebrities such as Steve Wozniak and John Dvorak as well as Apple representatives who explain new developments.

3.3.6.1.5
Apple User Groups Forum   **APPUG**

This forum is cosponsored with Apple Computer Incorporated. This is where Apple User Groups' officers can have direct contact with Apple. Along with the officers, members of user groups can meet and exchange information and newsletters. Individuals can also use this forum to find the Apple User Group closest to them.

3.3.6.1.6
Apples OnLine   **AOL**

Apples OnLine is a comprehensive electronic magazine for Apple users. This magazine contains updated information on various Apple users groups, their newsletters and other Apple related magazines. Some of the users groups and magazines represented include the Berkeley Macintosh Users Group (BMUG), Washington Apple Pi (WAP), the Apple III Newsletter and the Third Apple Users Group (TAUTALES).

3

3.3.6.2
ATARI Forums   SIGATARI
There are three forums devoted to Atari computers: the Atari 8-Bit Forum (GO ATARI8), the Atari 16-Bit Forum (GO ATARI16), the Atari Developers Forum (GO ATARIDEV) and ANTIC ONLINE (GO ANTIC), an electronic magazine.

3.3.6.2.1
ATARI 8-Bit Forum   ATARI8
The forum is not affiliated with Atari Corporation but is maintained by independent Forum Administrators (SysOps) and centers on the Atari 8-bit computer. The data libraries contain programs, text files, help information, product reviews and transcripts of previous conferences. The Forum Administrators and others in the forum are willing to help you and answer your questions.

3.3.6.2.2
ATARI 16-Bit Forum   ATARI16
This forum is similar to the Atari 8-Bit Forum but pertains to the ST-series (16-bit) Atari computers.

3.3.6.2.3
ATARI Developers Forum   ATARIDEV
This third Atari forum supports the special interests related to the development of software and hardware development for both the 8-bit and 16-bit lines of Atari computers.

3.3.6.2.4
ANTIC ONLINE   ANTIC
ANTIC ONLINE is the first online magazine exclusively for Atari computer users. Within this magazine you will find the latest Atari news, product surveys, letters to the editor and product reviews.

3.3.6.3
Commodore Users Network   CBMNET
There are five forums devoted to Commodore computers: the Amiga Forum (GO AMIGAFORUM), the Commodore Arts and Games Forum (GO CBMART), the Commodore Communications Forum (GO CBMCOM), the Commodore Programming Forum (GO CBMPRG) and the Commodore Service Forum (GO CBM2000).

3.3.6.3.1
Amiga Forum   **AMIGAFORUM**

The Amiga Forum offers news, information, ideas and programs for Commodore's Amiga personal computer. Anyone is welcome to participate in the Amiga Forum — Amiga owners, software developers, prospective owners, and people who are just interested in watching the development of a new computer.

3.3.6.3.2
Commodore Arts and Games Forum   **CBMART**

Commodore Arts and Games Forum is an interactive electronic forum dedicated to the support and dissemination of news. It includes public domain games, graphics and music for the Commodore 8-bit line of computers.

3.3.6.3.3
Commodore Communications Forum   **CBMCOM**

Commodore Communications Forum is an interactive electronic forum dedicated to the support, dissemination of news, discussions of information regarding software application programs, telecommunications and user-oriented topics for the Commodore 8-bit line of computers. It includes various public domain software.

3.3.6.3.4
Commodore Programming Forum   **CBMPRG**

The Commodore Programming Forum is an interactive forum dedicated to the support, dissemination, and discussion of information regarding the programming and technical aspects of the C-128, C-64, PET, VIC-20, and B128 computers, along with various public domain programs to aid the programmer in the techniques of programming.

3.3.6.3.4.5
Commodore Service Forum   **CBM2000**

Commodore Service Forum is a forum for direct customer service with Commodore. There are no data libraries but there are conferencing and a message board.

3.3.6.4
Computer Club Forum   **CLUB**

The Computer Club Forum is a club intended for people whose computer interests are not covered by other forums. Currently, the forum attracts Adam, Timex Sinclair, Sinclair QL, Eagle IIE, Sanyo and Actrix portable computer users, although users of other computer systems are always welcome.

3

3.3.6.5
DEC Users Network   **DECUNET**
The DEC Users Network is comprised of three forums: the DEC PC Forum (GO DECPC), the PDP-11 Forum (GO PDP11), and the VAX Forum (GO VAXSIG).

3.3.6.5.1
DEC PC Forum   **DECPC**
The DEC PC Forum is intended for users of Digital Equipment Corp. (DEC) personal computers. Members exchange information, ideas, public domain programs, and problems concerning DEC PCs with other members.

3.3.6.5.2
PDP-11 Forum   **PDP11**
This forum encourages the exchange of software designed to run on Digital Equipment Corporation's PDP/LSI computer systems and covers many languages used on PDPs including Macro, Fortran, Basic, Basic-Plus, "C", DIBOL & DBL, and Pascal. PDP-11 Users Group is designed to facilitate communication between users of the PDP-11, LSI-11, and PDP-10 series of computers.

3.3.6.5.3
VAX Forum   **VAXSIG**
The VAX Forum enables users of Digital Equipment Corporation's line of 32-bit computers to share information and ideas with other VAX users. A section of the forum is reserved for members who use the Unix operating system.

3.3.6.6
Epson Forum   **EPSON**
EpsOnLine provides Epson microcomputer/printer users with product information, technical assistance, public domain software, and a nationwide communications network. Also included are a message exchange area, database "reference libraries", and forums which offer the Epson user valuable technical insight into the product's use.

3.3.6.7
Heath Users Group (HUG)   **HEATHUSERS**
Heath Users Group's purpose is to further the exchange of information about Heath/Zenith computers in order to enhance and maintain their usefulness. The forum encourages information from Heath/Zenith users regarding software/peripheral functions. In addition, the field of robotics is discussed.

3.3.6.8
Hewlett-Packard PC Forum   HP

The Hewlett-Packard PC Forum is one component of Hewlett-Packard/Online, an online information service to help you achieve the most value from Hewlett-Packard personal computers. It is supported by Hewlett-Packard, and you can converse online with HP support engineers.

3.3.6.9
IBM Users Network   IBMNET

This forum is devoted to the topic of the IBM Personal Computer and IBM PC "compatibles." It includes the IBM New Users Forum (GO IBMNEW), IBM Communications Forum (GO IBMCOM), IBM Hardware Forum (GO IBMHW), IBM Junior Forum (GO IBMJR) and IBM Software Forum (GO IBMSW).

3.3.6.9.1
IBM New Users Forum   IBMNEW

If you are just getting started with your IBM, either in the world of communications or using the CompuServe forums, you might want to drop by this forum.

3.3.6.9.2
IBM Communications Forum   IBMCOM

This forum is devoted to the topic of telecommunications on the IBM Personal Computer and compatible computers.

3.3.6.9.3
IBM Hardware Forum   IBMHW

The major theme in the IBM Hardware Forum is the discussion of the various products available for the PC. The PC world changes rapidly and keeping up to date on new developments and sharing experiences with certain products make purchasing decisions easier. In the data libraries are hardware related programs and reviews of new and useful products.

3.3.6.9.4
IBM Junior Forum   IBMJR

Specific needs of the PCjr are addressed in this forum. It includes information on public domain programs and information relating to common problems, solutions and experiences.

3.3.6.9.5
IBM Software Forum   **IBMSW**
This forum is devoted to the topic of software on the IBM Personal Computer and any and all other compatible computers.

3.3.6.9.6
PC Vendor Support Forum   **PCVEN**
The PC Vendor Support Forum provides subscribers with support from multiple vendors of PC products. The vendors include ButtonWare (PC-File +, word processing, graphics and communication), Mansfield Software (KEDIT and REXX), the Software Group (Enable) and Broderbund (entertainment and productivity software).

3.3.6.10
Kaypro Users' Group   **KAYPRO**
Kaypro Forum enables Kaypro users to exchange information and assistance with other Kaypro users. There are 10 message areas and databases including information on products which can be added to Kaypro computers, hardware related files, and Help files which are designed to get the novice user off on the right foot.

3.3.6.11
Tandy Users Network   **TANDYNET**
The Tandy Users Network comprises eight Tandy product forums: the Color Computer Forum (GO COCO), the LDOS/TRSDOS6 Forum (GO LDOS), the Model 100/Portables Forum (GO M100SIG), the OS-9 Forum (GO OS9), the Tandy Professional Forum (GO TRS80PRO), the TANGENT Forum (GO TANGENT) and the Tandy Corporation Newsletter (GO TRS).

3.3.6.11.1
Color Computer Forum   **COCO**
The TRS-80 CoCo Users Group provides independent support for owners and operators of the TRS-80 Color Computer and related peripherals. Technical information, programming examples, and a forum where CoCo owners can meet and discuss problems and desires are also included.

3.3.6.11.2
LDOS/TRSDOS6 Forum   **LDOS**

The LDOS/TRSDOS6 Forum welcomes all users of the Radio Shack TRS-80 Models 1, 3, 4, 4P, 40, as well as users of "work-alike" computers such as the LOBO MAX-80. Topics discussed include BASIC, "C", Fortran, Ratfor, the Z-80 assembly language and the "hardware" of the TRS-80 product line. In addition, users of TRS-80 hardware and software, the LDOS 5.1 and TRSDOS6 operating systems can gain support.

3.3.6.11.3
Model 100 Forum   **M100SIG**

The Model 100 Forum is intended for the users of the TRS-80 Model 100. Subscribers can share knowledge, experiences, programs, and product information with other subscribers. There are 10 message board topics and databases which contain 1,000+ files of interest to Model 100 users. The data library and message board also support the Tandy 200 and NEC 8201A.

3.3.6.11.4
OS-9 Forum   **OS9**

The OS9 Operating System Forum is dedicated to users of the OS9 operating system. The forum contains programs, utilities, data files, hints, tips, and discussions that pertain to OS9.

3.3.6.11.5
Tandy Professional Forum   **TRS80PRO**

The Tandy Professional Forum offers Tandy computer users an avenue for exchange of information with other subscribers regarding the full line of Tandy computers.

3.3.6.11.6
TANGENT Forum   **TANGENT**

TANGENT is the forum for business users of Tandy computers. Members have access to up-to-date technical information, support and input. You can keep informed through bulletins, public message boards, conferences and member discussions. Data libraries contain downloadable public domain software, product reviews, reports and journal abstracts. The emphasis in this forum is on the Tandy Model 2/12/16/600 line of equipment but, of course, everyone is welcome.

3.3.6.11.7
Tandy Corporation Newsletter   TRS
Tandy Newsletter is designed to keep Tandy computer users informed of current activities within the Tandy corporation. In addition, you have access to a conference schedule and Tandy product and technical information.

3.3.6.12
Telecommunications Forum   TELECOMM
The Telecommunications Forum is dedicated to microcomputer telecommunications. Subjects under discussion include BBSing, downloading from CompuServe, terminal software, packet networks, and micro-to-mainframe links. Subscribers may also refer to the Telecommunications Forum when seeking information about problems regarding a particular modem or information service.

3.3.6.13
Texas Instruments News   TINEWS
Texas Instruments News is a menu-driven, text area where complete forum instructions, help with tricky file transfers, the latest forum news, and forum feedback can be found.

3.3.6.13.5
Texas Instruments Forum   TIFORUM
The Texas Instruments Forum is for anyone interested in any model of Texas Instruments brand computers especially the TI-99/4A and TI Professional. The TI Forum has an active message base and rapidly expanding data libraries. Weekly conferences are also scheduled.

Members and Forum Administrators (SysOps) will be happy to assist new subscribers. The TI Forum is now a major source of TI information across the country, supplementing a local users group network and bulletin board systems.

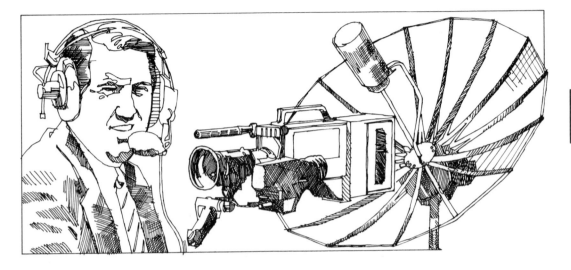

3.3.7
Media/Electronic Publishing   **PCS-100**
These forums are for people who are interested in communications — written, broadcast and electronic.

3.3.7.1
AI EXPERT Magazine   **AIE**
AI Expert is a forum for readers of *AI Expert Magazine* and those interested in artificial intelligence. In this forum, you can query industry and academic leaders in the AI field as well as exchange AI information with other members. As a member, you have access to public domain expert systems and software. Articles, bibliographies, news, and product reviews are available in human readable form.

3.3.7.2
Broadcast Professional Forum   **BPFORUM**
Broadcast Professional Forum covers the major publications, manufacturers and trade associations, conventions, organizations, and seminars which relate to the fields of broadcast and audio engineering, production, and land mobile communications. Also included is the latest FCC news as it relates to the broadcast and communications professions.

3

3.3.7.3
Computer Language Magazine   CLM

The Computer Language Magazine is a gathering place for professionals and serious amateurs who are fluent in two or more computer languages. Discussions center on the merits of various languages as well as topics of interest to the professional programmer. It serves as a distribution center for programs referred to in the print version of the magazine.

3.3.7.4
Dr. Dobb's Journal Forum   DDJFORUM

Dr. Dobb's Journal is a magazine devoted to programming languages, techniques, tools, utilities, and algorithms. The DDJ Forum is the electronic extension of the magazine. The primary purpose of the forum is to make available in electronic form the programming code published every month in the pages of the magazine (GO DDJ). The forum is also intended to stimulate discussion between journal readers and editors/authors/columnists and to serve as a general clearinghouse for information of interest to professional programmers.

3.3.7.5.1
Family Computing Forum   FAMFORUM

The Family Computing Forum members can discuss issues related to computing in the home and how it affects the family. Data libraries contain articles of special interest and members are encouraged to contribute their own.

3.3.7.5.2
Computer Club Forum   CLUB
Refer to 3.3.6.4

3.3.7.6
Journalism Forum   JFORUM

Journalism Forum serves the professional journalist with a variety of services and specialized data libraries. Journalism Forum offers separate data libraries for Radio, TV, Print and Photo/Video Journalists. In addition, there are data libraries dedicated to jobs listings, freelance opportunities, equipment exchanges, commentary, and a listing of names and phone numbers of proven resources.

3.3.8
Home/Health/Family Forums   HOM-50

This section contains forums where people share their ideas on topics that enrich lives such as religion, music, politics and sexuality.

3.3.8.1
Aquaria/Fish Forum   FISHNET

Aquarium professionals and hobbyists alike can join the Aquaria & Tropical Fish Forum to talk "fish." Members of fish specialty groups can exchange information on products, diseases and news. Join a live conference and meet fellow fish fanciers across the country.

Regular conferences are scheduled with some of the nation's best known aquarists. Questions to the Forum Administrator (SysOp) will be answered within 24 hours, but if you can't wait, a voice line is available.

3.3.8.2
Religion Forum   RELIGION

The Religion Forum is designed for people who like to share discussions, opinions and information, as well as ask questions, on topics which relate to religion. Forum members may meet new "friends" while expanding their theological horizons.

3.3.8.3
Working from Home Forum   WORK
The Working From Home Forum unites those who work from their homes with others who are in similar circumstances. It allows a subscriber to exchange information, make contacts, share resources and solutions to problems and meet other subscribers, as well as keep up-to-date on the latest home/office management tips, resources, laws, tax benefits, and marketing approaches.

3.3.8.4
National Issues/People Forum   ISSUESFORUM
The National Issues/People Forum is a forum for the free exchange of ideas about current issues and names in the news. There are sections for discussion of peace, politics, individualism, high tech, handicapped, paranormal, men and women's issues, youth and social issues. A number of regularly-scheduled conferences are held, and the data libraries contain many interesting articles, message threads and conference transcripts.

3.3.8.5
Military Veterans Services   VET
The Military Vets Forum encourages discussion of current topics, and includes a personal adjustment section for Vets to inquire about problems, data library files on veterans benefits, the MIA/POW issue, Agent Orange, Atomic Vets, Veterans Organizations and member writings. The complete list of the names on the Vietnam Veterans Memorial and a direct connection to CDC on the Agent Orange Studies is included. A CompuServe Forum and Buddy Locator are available to veterans only.

3.3.8.6
RockNet   ROCK
Refer to 3.3.4.7

3.3.8.6.5
RockNet (Rock Music) Forum   ROCKNET
Refer to 3.3.4.7.5

3.3.8.7
Food/Wine Forums   FOOD
This section contains forums for people who enjoy good food and wine.

3.3.8.7.1
Cook's Online **COOKS**

This is a place where people can share their enthusiasm for cooking and gourmet food. Members swap recipes, exchange cooking tips and share menu planning ideas. Fine restaurants are discussed and members can consult with cooking experts online.

3.3.8.7.2
Bacchus Wine Forum **WINEFORUM**

The Bacchus Wine Forum presents information on many wine-related topics. Information about your favorite wines may also be shared with other winelovers. Issues of *The Informed Enophile*, a wine newsletter, are included, and online wine-tasting parties are held regularly.

3.3.8.8
HamNet (Ham Radio) Online **HAM**

Refer to 3.3.3.5

3.3.8.8.3
HamNet (Ham Radio) Forum **HAMNET**

Refer to 3.3.3.5.3

3.3.8.9
Auto Racing Forum **RACING**

Auto Racing Forum provides the subscriber with driver biographies, track information, sanctioning organization addresses and contact information, schedules, and other information of interest to motorsports fans. In addition, real-time auto racing reports, filed directly from major events across the United States and Canada, are included.

3.3.8.10
ModelNet **MODELNET**

Refer to 3.3.1.2

3

3.3.8.11
Human Sexuality Forum   **HUMAN**

Human sexuality questions and problems are answered in an informative manner. Special features include articles on social skills, dating, relationships and sexual problems. Experts answer questions on a variety of topics. Two forums are available for subscribers to share their feelings, experiences and relationships with others in a warm, supportive environment.

3.3.8.11.5.1
HSX Support Group A   **HSX-100**

This forum is geared toward specific groups such as couples, parents, singles, women and gays.

3.3.8.11.5.2
HSX Support Group B   **HSX-200**

This forum focuses on specific topics such as passages, breaking up, encounter groups and bisexuality.

3.3.8.12
Sci-Fi/Fantasy   **SCI**
Refer to 3.3.3.9

3.3.8.12.1
Sci-Fi/Fantasy Forum   **SCI-FI**
Refer to 3.3.3.9.1

3.3.8.12.2
Comic Book Forum   **COMIC**
Refer to 3.3.3.9.2

3.3.8.13
General Music Forum   **MUSICFORUM**
Refer to 3.3.4.5

3.3.8.14
Good Earth Forum   GOODEARTH

The Good Earth Forum provides a place for subscribers to discuss topics which relate to natural living. Topics include gardening, horticulture, natural nutrition, and folkways. In addition, the forum provides a section for those who speak and write Esperanto.

3.3.8.15
Literary Forum   LITFORUM

The Literary Forum is a gathering place for professional writers, literature readers, journalists, humorists, and those with an interest in any related field. Included are sections on poetry, controversial topics, fiction discussions, science fiction, comics, humor and journalism.

3

3.3.8.16
Outdoor Forum   OUTDOORFORUM

The Great Outdoors provides outdoor lovers with an avenue to converse and share information with other outdoor lovers. Areas and topics of information include camping, climbing, backpacking, fishing, hunting, cycling, sailing, and winter sports. In addition, search and rescue, nature, wildlife, equipment reviews and park and campground information is included.

3.3.8.17
Consumer Electronics Forum   CEFORUM

Refer to 3.3.3.4

3.3.8.18
Healthcom/Health Forum   HCM

Healthcom/Health Forum allows a subscriber to discuss health-related matters with other subscribers including topics on mental health, child care and sexuality. Subscribers also have access to biomedical literature through MEDLINE as well as current and accurate information on rare disorders and diseases through the NORD Services/Rare Disease Database. In addition, an AIDS quiz and AIDS reference library are available.

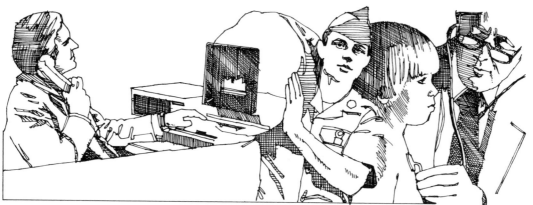

3.3.9
Professional Forums   **PROFORUM**

This section contains forums for lawyers, doctors and other professionals and those interested in professional fields.

3.3.9.1
PR and Marketing Forum   **PRSIG**

The Public Relations and Marketing Forum provides a special interest group for professional communicators such as public relations, marketing and communications directors or those holding related jobs in the public and private sector. The data libraries cover a wide variety of topics as they relate to PR including government, education, public affairs, financial institutions, consumer affairs, computers, high tech, health/social services and PRSA. The teleconferences enable a member to hear from recognized communications experts. In addition, the forum may be used to establish meetings by members for specific reasons.

3.3.9.2
Legal Forum   **LAWSIG**

The Legal Forum is designed specifically for attorneys, police, corrections officers, paralegals and laypersons interested in the law. Topics such as copyrights, bankruptcy, software/hardware for the law office, Lexis vs Westlaw, pros and cons of polygraph tests, fingerprinting children and other law-related subjects are debated.

3.3.9.3
AAMSI Medical Forum   **MEDSIG**

AAMSI is sponsored by the Amerrican Association for Medical Systems and Informatics. Members represent all segments of the professional medical community and use this forum to exchange ideas and information on medically-related topics.

3.3.9.4
Safetynet   **SAFETYNET**

The Safetynet Forum provides an area where anyone interested in safety-related issues can post messages, participate in teleconferencing, and receive information from the data libraries. Topics covered include regulations and standards, chemical and physical hazards, hazardous materials, fire services/prevention/investigation, and emergency medical services.

3.3.9.5
Autodesk Forum   **ADESK**

Autodesk is a computer-aided design (CAD) software forum. It offers information on Autodesk products, applications programs, usage tips, and product support. Autodesk provides a worldwide meeting place for AutoCAD users, dealers, peripheral manufacturers, applications developers, and Autodesk staff.

3.3.9.7
Computer Training Forum   **DPTRAIN**

Refer to 3.3.2.3

3.3.9.8
Military Veterans Forum   **VETSIG**

This forum enables veterans to gain and exchange information. It includes information on veterans benefits, Vietnam veterans information and a buddy locator service.

3.3.9.10
Computer Consultant's Forum   **CONSULT**

The Computer Consultant's Forum is the place for computer consultants to exchange ideas and information on networks, product vendors, commercial software and equipment. Independent consultants can share business tips, technical information and solutions to client problems. The forum is sponsored by the Independent Computer Consultants Association (ICCA), which represents data processing professionals.

3.3.9.11
Health Forum   **GOODHEALTH**

Health Forum provides the subscriber with general health-related information. Included are discussions on fitness and emotional and family health. Every Friday night a "Trivia Night" is held where the professional or non-professional may answer health-related questions.

3.3.9.12
Int'l Entrepreneurs Network   **USEN**

The Int'l Entrepreneurs Network is an information exchange for entrepreneurs and business resources. Topics discussed include business start up procedures and the development of entrepreneurship. Members are encouraged to discuss business related problems, ideas and techniques.

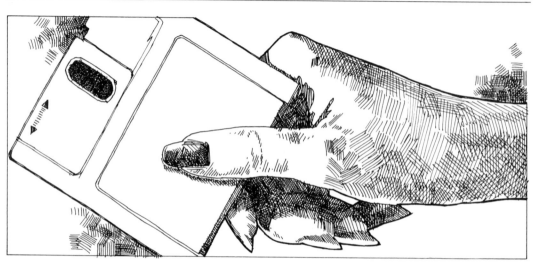

3.3.10
Software Forums   **SOFTWARE**

Software Forums enable the users of different software packages to exchange ideas and solutions to problems. Some forums are supported by the software publishers.

3.3.10.1
AI EXPERT Forum   **AIE**

Refer to 3.3.7.1

3.3.10.2
Aldus Forum   **ALDUS**

If you're interested in desktop publishing and Aldus Pagemaker, you'll want to join the Aldus Forum. In addition to idea exchanges with other users, detailed information on new product releases is available. Libraries contain technical support notes, templates for design formatting, and downloadable public domain and shareware programs. Aldus Forum is operated by the Aldus technical support staff who will answer your questions within 24 hours.

3.3.10.3
Ashton-Tate Support Library   **ASHTON**

The Ashton-Tate Support Library is an easy-to-use, menu-driven reference center and forum for users of dBase II and III, Framework and Multimate. The library is maintained by the A-T Software Support Center, which provide new product updates and announcements. The Ashton-Tate Forum (GO ASHFORUM) and monthly user surveys give members a direct line to A-T decision makers.

3.3.10.3.7
Ashton-Tate Forum   **ASHFORUM**

The Ashton-Tate Forum provides users of Ashton-Tate products with support from the Ashton-Tate Support Center. Subscribers can also exchange information, ideas, and solutions with other Ashton-Tate users. In addition, sample programs and usage articles for each of Ashton-Tate's major products are available. You can also find information on specific problems immediately in the Ashton-Tate support library (GO ASHTON).

3.3.10.4
Autodesk Forum   **ADESK**

Refer to 3.3.9.5

3.3.10.5
Borland International   **BORLAND**

The Borland International Forum enables users of Borland software to exchange information and discuss programming with other users of Borland software. Included are sections on Turbo Pascal, Sidekick and Superkey.

3.3.10.5.7
Borland Language Products Forum   **BORPRO**

If you are interested in learning more about programming with Turbo Pascal, Turbo Prolog, or other Borland International products, explore the Borland Language Products Forum. In this forum, you can participate in discussions with other members concerning these products and receive help from them. You can also work with other members on joint online projects.

3.3.10.5.8
Borland Application Products Forum   **BROAPP**

The Borland Application Products Forum is for users of the Borland Application Products — SideKick, SuperKey, Turbo Lightning, and Reflex. Members can talk to other members or ask technical questions from the Borland Technical Support Representatives. Data Libraries contain patches, enhancement programs, and product information.

3.3.10.6
CADRE Forum   **CADRE**
The CADRE Forum is for users of Applied Data Research (ADR) products such as ROSCOE, VOLLIE, IDEAL, ETC and EMAIL. Members can have debates, exchange messages, and participate in live conferences. Bulletins keep members informed about the CADRE Forum and coming events. Data libraries contain reports, software, spreadsheets and product reviews.

3.3.10.7
Computer Consultant's Forum   **CONSULT**
Refer to 3.3.9.10

3.3.10.8
Computer Language Magazine   **CLM**
Refer to 3.3.7.3

3.3.10.9
CP/M Forum   **CPMSIG**
The CP/M Forum is dedicated to users of the CP/M 8-bit and 16-bit computer operating systems. Subscribers exchange information and discuss problems with other CP/M users. In addition to discussing CP/M itself, programs which run on CP/M computers such as word processors and database programs are discussed.

3.3.10.10
Digital Research, Incorporated   **DRI**
Digital Research Forum includes Digital database and product information in addition to Digital Research news and current events. You can also find information on Digital Research dealers, warranty support, and a retail price list in this section.

3.3.10.10.7
Digital Research Forum   **DRFORUM**
Digital Research Forum is a professional forum for Digital Research end users and software developers. Topics cover application notes and patches, concurrent operating system information and graphics. In addition, end user support and information is available.

3.3.10.11
Dr. Dobb's Journal Magazine   **DDJ**
In the electronic edition of Dr. Dobb's Journal, you can gather information about computer languages, tools, utilities, algorithms, and programming techniques. In addition, reviews of commercial software development tools and libraries available to the professional micro-computer programmer are presented. You may also submit articles which will be reviewed for use in future publications.

3.3.10.12.1
Family Computing Forum   **FAMFORUM**
Refer to 3.3.7.5.1

3.3.10.12.2
Computer Club Forum   **CLUB**
Refer to 3.3.6.4

3.3.10.13
Forth Forum/Creative Solutions   **FORTH**
This forum is sponsored by Creative Solutions, Inc., to support its Forth products and to answer all general Forth questions. Forth is a powerful but compact programming language well-loved by programmers.

3.3.10.14
Javelin Forum   **JAVELIN**
Refer to 3.3.5.4

3.3.10.15
LDOS/TRSDOS6 Forum   **LDOS**
Refer to 3.3.6.11.2

3.3.10.16
Living Videotext Forum   **LVTFORUM**
Living Videotext (LVT) is the developer and publisher of ThinkTank, Ready!, and MORE. Living Videotext Forum was established to give support to users of idea-processing soft-ware products. You can give your ideas, questions, or suggestions directly to the president of LVT.

3

3.3.10.17
LOGO Forum   **LOGOFORUM**
Refer to 3.3.2.8

3.3.10.18
MicroPro Forum   **MICROPRO**
The MicroPro Forum provides a medium for users of MicroPro software such as WordStar, WordStar 2000, InfoStar and CalcStar to interact with other MicroPro software users. The forum is organized into sub-topics for each of the product groups as well as a section for discussion of printers and one for Apple computers. In addition, an Add-On Products section is available where subscribers may discuss and review products developed by other companies for use with MicroPro software.

3.3.10.19
Microsoft Connection   **MSCON**
The Microsoft Connection is operated by the Microsoft Product Support Group for all users of their software. Members can ask questions directly to Microsoft or share information with other members. The common questions and answers section may resolve your problem on the spot. Additional features include product release announcements, training information, and a directory of Microsoft centers around the world.

3.3.10.19.6
Microsoft Forum   **MSOFT**
The Microsoft Users Group provides a forum where users can communicate with Microsoft, to ask questions about various Microsoft products and receive product information.

3.3.10.20
Monogram Software Forum   **MONOGRAM**
Refer to 3.3.5.9

3.3.10.21
OS-9 Forum   **OS-9**
Refer to 3.3.6.11.4

3.3.10.22
Pascal (MUSUS)   **MUSUS**
The Pascal (MUSUS) Forum is a membership benefit of USUS, Inc., the UCSD Pascal
System User Society. Through MUSUS, members of USUS exchange information on a
variety of topics, mostly centered on use of the UCSD Pascal, Apple Pascal and similar
software systems.

3.3.10.23
Programmers' Forum   **PROSIG**
The Programmers Forum is for anyone who is interested in programming computers,
whether beginner or expert. If it has to do with programming, it is likely that one of the
members has had experience with it and can save you money, time and frustration by
steering you away from a bad product or idea or towards a good one. The data libraries
contain numerous programs and even computer humor.

3.3.10.24
Software Publishing Online   **SPC**
The Software Publishing Company was started by individuals who believe that busy professionals need productivity tools that are quickly learned. Thus, SPC developed a family
of integrated products that stress simple functionality. Their PFS (Personal Filing System)
line includes a filing system, a report writer, a word processor and planner. Their Harvard
Software line consists of project management software and the Harvard Professional Publisher. Subscribers can join the Software Publishing Forum to exchange ideas on SPC
products and to keep up with the latest developments.

3.3.10.24.5
Software Publishing Forum   **SPCFORUM**
The Software Publishing Forum is designed to get technical and product information to its
members. The data libraries contain information on individual products as well as valuable
templates to be used with PFS software.

3.3.10.25
Whole Earth Software   **WHOLEEARTH**
The Whole Earth Software Forum offers subscribers information on the best resources
available for computer-oriented and non-computer-oriented purposes. Topics include reviews and recommendations of computer software, computer conferencing and telecommunications, the health hazards of computers, and the general effects of computers on people. In addition, the online publication of the Whole Earth Chronicle Column, a weekly
guide to recommended tools and ideas, is included.

3.3.10.26
World of Lotus   **LOTUS**

The World of Lotus is sponsored and maintained by the Lotus Development Corporation to provide support to users of Lotus products and information about Lotus products and services. It includes news releases and other company information from Lotus, a list of software books and periodicals that complement Lotus products, technical product information, and answers to commonly asked questions. It provides "electronic distribution" of new device drivers, problem fixes and other technical information. Also included in the World of Lotus are the 1-2-3 Users Forum, the Symphony Users Forum, and the Jazz Users Forum all of which feature communication with Lotus product support as well as with other Lotus users.

3.3.10.26.6
Lotus 1-2-3 User Forum   **LOTUS123**
Refer to 3.3.5.5

3.3.10.26.7
Lotus Symphony User Forum   **SYMPHONY**
Refer to 3.3.5.8

3.3.10.26.8
Lotus Graphics Products   **LOTUSGRAPHIC**
Refer to 3.3.5.6

3.3.10.26.9
Lotus Jazz Forum   **LOTUSJAZZ**
Refer to 3.3.5.7

3.3.11
Sports Forums   **COM-13**
Do you like to talk baseball or auto racing? Then stop by one of the sports forums to discuss these or other sports.

3.3.11.1
Auto Racing Forum   **RACING**
Refer to 3.3.8.9

3.3.11.2
Sports Forum   **FANS**
The Sports Forum includes discussions on the NFL, major league baseball, NHL hockey and NBA basketball. Topics include trade rumors, performances and injuries of upcoming opponents, and possible franchise moves. A baseball simulation league is also available to the subscriber.

3.3.12
Travel Forums   **TRA-11**
Do you want to go where the sun keeps shining, the sights are spectacular, or natives are delightful? Then visit one of the travel forums to exchange ideas with fellow travelers.

3.3.12.1
Travel Forum   **TRAVSIG**

The Travel Forum allows those interested in travel to swap stories, ideas, and information with other forum members. You can talk with others who have already been to your destination to find out the best (or worst) restaurants and hotels. You can learn about the customs in foreign countries and other important information. You can also find out about destination spots and cruises. Leave questions for others or share your experiences.

3.3.12.2
Florida Forum   **FLORIDA**

The Florida Forum allows residents, vacationers or anyone with an interest in Florida to share information about the sunshine state. You can talk with the residents to find out the best places to stay, eat, or visit if you're planning a vacation. Find information on sporting and recreational activities in the Florida state or events/attractions of interest. A Travel and Trivia Contest is held every week in the forum and guest speakers appear often in the online conferences.

3.3.13
Comic Book Forum   **COMIC**
Refer to 3.3.3.9.2

3.4
National Bulletin Board   **BULLETIN**

This Bulletin Board contains information posted by subscribers. It has three categories of information - items for SALE, services WANTED and general NOTICES. You can read bulletins from other subscribers or post your own.

3.5
Subscriber Directory   **DIRECTORY**

The CompuServe Subscriber Directory enables you to search for other subscribers by name. All subscribers are included in the Subscriber Directory, unless they specifically request exclusion. Now you can obtain the User ID number of other subscribers and easily communicate with them via EasyPlex or through our other online communication services.

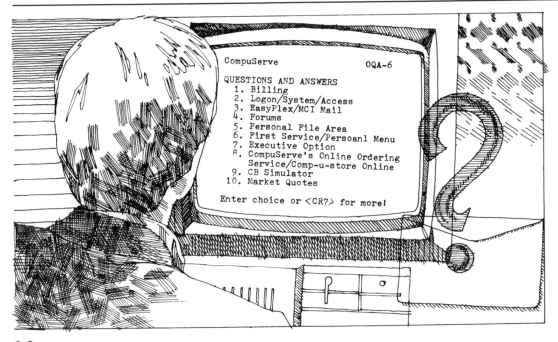

```
CompuServe                    OQA-6

QUESTIONS AND ANSWERS
  1. Billing
  2. Logon/System/Access
  3. EasyPlex/MCI Mail
  4. Forums
  5. Personal File Area
  6. First Service/Persoanl Menu
  7. Executive Option
  8. CompuServe's Online Ordering
     Service/Comp-u-store Online
  9. CB Simulator
 10. Market Quotes

Enter choice or <CR7> for more!
```

3.6
Ask Customer Service   QUESTION

Customer Service makes it easy to get the help you need whenever you need it.

When a question comes up while you're online, type GO QUESTION to visit the Questions and Answers service. Customer Service provides a list of commonly asked questions about CompuServe and their answers. Questions are answered on such topics as EasyPlex, billing, forums, logon, CB and VIDTEX. Customer Service is continually updating the Questions and Answers database to keep up with the growing Information Service.

When you can't find the assistance you need in users guides or online, let Customer Service answer your individual questions. Customer Service representatives help subscribers solve any problems they may encounter and encourage their comments. Type GO FEEDBACK to visit the Feedback area to send questions, comments or suggestions to CompuServe.

If you have a question or problem that requires immediate attention, such as logging on, a Customer Service Representative can help you. Subscribers within Ohio and from outside the U.S. can call (614) 457-8650. Subscribers from outside Ohio and within the U.S. including Hawaii, Alaska, Puerto Rico, St. Thomas, St. John and St. Croix can call (800) 848-8990. Representatives are generally available from 8 A.M. to midnight, Monday through Friday and from 2 P.M. to midnight on weekends, Eastern Time. Holiday hours vary.

3.6.2
Feedback to CompuServe   **FEEDBACK**
Feedback enables you to send your question, comment or suggestion to CompuServe.
Your connect time is free while you are in FEEDBACK, although you will still be charged
for any communication surcharges. You'll be told upon exiting FEEDBACK when connect
charges resume.
     The Customer Service Representative will answer via EasyPlex as quickly as possible.

3.7
CB Society — Cupcake's Column   **CUPCAKE**
Refer to 3.2.5

3.8
Access (Public File Area)   **ACCESS**
Access (Public File Area) allows you to browse, scan, download, upload, and read files in
the public file area. In addition, you can copy files from the public file area to your personal file area.

3.9 Convention Center   **CONVENTION**
The Electronic Convention Center^{SM} allows subscribers to access any of CompuServe's
special conferences from one place. You can view information on scheduled conferences
and decide if you would like to attend. Information about each conference is displayed:
general description, conference type, date and time, expected length and whether a
reservation is required. A reservation, if needed, can be made at that time.

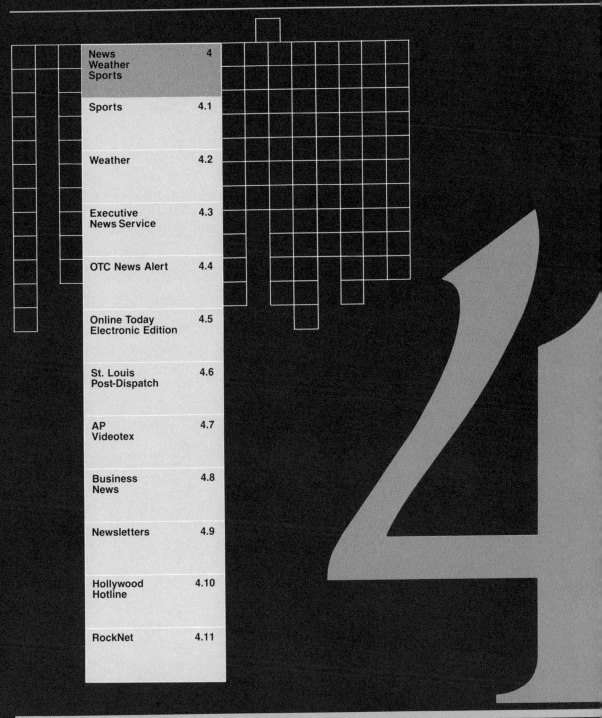

This chapter contains the latest news including sports scores updated throughout the game, aviation weather, feature stories, business news, newsletters, and even Hollywood gossip. Some of the products have compiled extensive databases and statistics including win/loss records, point spreads, etc. The chapter even includes some games.

4.1
Sports   **SPORTS**

This section includes sports news, games and other sports information.

4.1.1
Associated Press Sports   **APV-5**

The Associated Press Sports Wire gives the latest scores, news and league leaders in football, baseball, basketball, soccer, hockey, tennis and golf as well as information on college sports.

4.1.2
Sports Forum   **FANS**

The Sports Forum includes discussions on the NFL, major league baseball, NHL hockey and NBA basketball. Topics include trade rumors, performances and injuries of upcoming opponents, and possible franchise moves. A baseball simulation league is also available to the subscriber.

4.1.3
Auto Racing Forum   RACING

Auto Racing Forum provides the subscriber with driver biographies, track information, sanctioning organization addresses and contact information, schedules, and other information of interest to motorsports fans. In addition, real-time auto racing reports, filed directly from major events across the United States and Canada, are included.

4.1.4
Sports Medicine   HRF-4794

Jog, bike, swim, or ski to the Sports Medicine clinic. Information is available on basic exercise physiology, exercise testing, training, nutrition, and the general risks versus benefits of exercise. Articles discussing specific sports give information on each sport's benefits, advantages, disadvantages and information on how to get started. You can keep track of your fitness efforts using the chart of energy costs for various activities.

4.1.5
Simulation/Sports Games   SSGAMES

Simulated games of football, golf and air traffic controller provide excitement for competitive players to test their skills from the comfort of their own terminals.

4.1.5.1
Advanced Digital Football   ADFL

Armchair athletes, push aside that popcorn. The Digital Football League has drafted you to coach your team in a simulated contest. You can select your team, your opponent, and level of coaching involvement. You can call offensive and defensive plays using established strategies, or be creative and invent your own.

4.1.5.2
Air Traffic Controller   ATCONTROL

If you have nerves of steel and like the challenge of thinking at several levels at once, Air Traffic Controller could be your game. As an ATC, you're responsible for all planes within your sector of airspace. The object is to keep them from running out of fuel or crashing.

You must clear planes for arrival and landing while keeping track of those arriving from other sectors. Neighboring sectors may be controlled by other ATC players, challenging your communication skills as well as your nerves. Once you've built up your confidence, you can start again at an increased level of difficulty.

4.1.5.3
Football   **FOOTBALL**

It's fourth down and goal-to-go on the three-yard line. You're the coach for the offense. What play will you call? This is a situation you might encounter when playing CompuServe's version of Football. It can be played by one person or by two people at the same computer; you always play offense, while the computer plays defense. No matter who you're playing, you can never quite predict what they'll do.

4.1.5.4
Golf   **GOLF**

The average golfer must travel to a golf course to play. You, however, can play at your terminal on a championship 18-hole simulated layout. Your talent will lie in your intelligence, knowledge of the game, and your ability to keep your eye on the computerized ball.

4

4.1.6
The Great Outdoors   **OUTDOORFORUM**

The Great Outdoors provides outdoor lovers with an avenue to converse and share information with other outdoor lovers. Areas and topics of information include camping, climbing, backpacking, fishing, hunting, cycling, sailing, and winter sports. In addition, search and rescue, nature, wildlife, equipment reviews and park and campground information is included.

4.1.7
Computer Sports World   **CSW**

Computer Sports World is a division of Chronicle Information Services of San Francisco. It has compiled extensive files of sports information and some of their files are available here. Information available includes scores, schedules, standings, matchups, the Las Vegas Line and statistics. They also explain matchups and the statistics.

4.1.8
Sailing Forum   **SAILING**

Ahoy sailors! Sea dogs interested in staying downwind of current events should join the Sailing Forum. Members will share information and opinions about all aspects of sailing including equipment, racing, and favorite cruising spots.

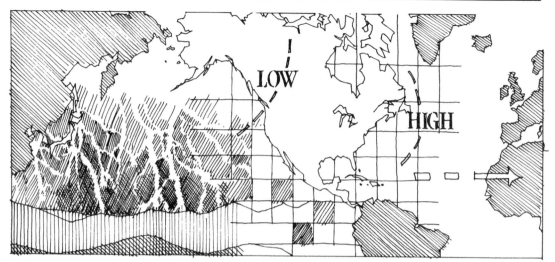

4.2
Weather   **WEATHER**
This section contains various weather products. See also topics under Aviation
(GO AVIATION).

4.2.1
NWS Public Weather   **WEA**
A continuously updated weather service featuring local city forecasts, state forecasts,
precipitation probability, marine and sports forecasts, and weather warnings. An entire
weather section is also available (GO AWX). **$***

4.2.2
AP Videotex Weather   **APV**
The latest news from Associated Press updated hourly. AP Weather contains the previous
day's HIGH and LOW for international locations. For U.S. locations, both today's and
tomorrow's HIGH, LOW and outlook forecasts are given.

4.2.3
NWS Aviation Weather   **AWX**
CompuServe Aviation Weather is instant weather for pilots. It uses the N.O.A.A. Service
"A" weather wire. This is the same data used in International Flight Service stations. Most
of the data is coded but is easy to read with a little practice. It includes hourly reports,
terminal forecasts, NOTAMS, PIREPS, SIGMETS, AIRMETS, area forecasts and radar
summaries. Updated continuously. **$**

4.2.4
VIDTEX Weather Maps   **MAPS**

These weather maps can be displayed on most computers running CompuServe's VIDTEX terminal software or using one of the free public-domain graphics decoders from the Aviation Forum. They include a national map, surface synoptic map, and an aviation weather depiction chart. These maps are black and white only. **$**

4.3
Executive News Service   **ENS**

Executive News Service is the unique electronic clipping service that monitors Associated Press news wires, the Washington Post, OTC NewsAlert and Reuters for stories of interest to you. Stories containing words or phrases you specify are clipped as they come across the wires and held in electronic folders for you to review at your convenience. You are also able to forward these stories to others (or yourself) through EasyPlex. **$E**

4

4.4
OTC NewsAlert   **OTCNEWS**

OTC NewsAlert is a database and clipping service that tracks activities that could affect stock prices of all large and small companies whose stocks trade over-the-counter. Investors, corporate information officers, and competitors can search both recent and historic articles featuring summary earning reports, large sales contracts, new products, acquisitions, takeovers, movements of large blocks of stocks by corporate insiders, and attempts to take companies private. Also included is information on initial public offerings. Information is obtained from a variety of news services, from filings with the Securities and Exchange Commission, and from the companies themselves. OTC NewsAlert items can be searched by company name, stock symbol or topic. A clipping file can be set up through the Executive News Service to follow individual company and industry trends. E

4.5
Online Today Electronic Edition   **OLT**

The Electronic Edition of CompuServe's *Online Today* magazine. The *Online Today Electronic Edition* provides daily updated computer and information industry news, CompuServe news, product announcements, reviews of new hardware, software, books and more.

4.6
St. Louis Post-Dispatch   **SPD**

The *St. Louis Post-Dispatch* supplies news events from the Associated Press. Categories include Washington News, National News, World News, Sports and Financial News. Updated hourly.

4.7
AP Videotex   **APV**

The latest news from Associated Press updated hourly. It includes weather, national news, Washington news, world news, political happenings, entertainment, business news, Wall Street news, Dow Jones averages, features, sports and today in history.

4.8
Business News   **BUSNEWS**

This section contains business news services. It is a way for the busy executive to catch up on the latest business news.

4.8.1
AP Videotex   **APV**

Refer to 4.7

4.8.2
Online Today Electronic Edition   **OLT**

Refer to 4.5

4.8.4
The Business Wire   TBW

The Business Wire makes available press releases, news articles and other information from the world of business. It is updated continuously throughout the day and brings information on hundreds of different companies.

4.9
Newsletters   **NEWSLETTERS**

This product contains a collections of newsletters.

4.9.2
ASI's Biweekly Monitor   **ASI**

Aviation Safety Institute provides information on a variety of safety-related topics. Topics include Service Difficulty Reports and Hazard Reports, along with articles on flight operations, human factors, airport reviews and safety tips. The information in ASI Monitor, an online newsletter, is updated monthly.

4.9.3
Commodore Information Network   **CBM**

The Commodore Information Network contains information relevant to Commodore computer users and gives you a place to meet other subscribers to exchange ideas and information.

4.9.4
Tandy Newsletter   **TRS**

Tandy Newsletter is designed to keep Tandy computer users informed of current activities within the Tandy corporation. In addition, you have access to a conference schedule and Tandy product and technical information.

4.10
Hollywood Hotline   **HOLLYWOOD**

Hollywood Hotline is a news and information service of noteworthy events in motion pictures, television programs and music recordings. It also includes a trivia quiz, entertainment features, photos of stars (GO HHA), and an entertainment encyclopedia which includes such things as past Academy and Tony award winners. Also included in this product are the movie reviewettes (GO MOVIES) and the SHOWBIZQUIZ (GO SHOWBIZ). To receive the photos you must be using VIDTEX or similar software with a computer with high resolution graphic capabilities. Updated daily. **$**

4.11
RockNet　　　　　　　　　　　　　　　　　　**ROCK**

RockNet provides the music enthusiast with up-to-the-minute news and information on the world of rock. It contains:

- The RockNet Forum (GO ROCKNET),
- Rock news,
- A list of top record reviews and
- Articles about rock music.

4.11.5
RockNet Forum　　　　　　　　　　　　　**ROCKNET**

The RockNet Forum has many members that are within the record industry, and you may learn news items before they appear in newspapers.

The Travel and Leisure chapter provides you with air, hotel, car, tour and cruise information. In addition, U.S. domestic and international information is available.

5.1
What's New in Travel   **WNT**

What's New in Travel is an online guide to CompuServe's Travel Services including a guided tour to the various travel services available and a travel index to help you easily find the information and services you're looking for. What's New in Travel also keeps you continuously updated on new enhancements to the travel products, new services, contests, promotions and more. There's also a section listing reduced packages, discounts and special services you are entitled to as a CompuServe subscriber. You'll want to check this area often as it changes frequently.

5.1.6
Adventures in Travel   **AIT**

Adventures in Travel contains travel articles covering all aspects of travel all over the world. Articles are written by travel writer Lee Foster and other professional travel writers. New articles appear every two weeks and you may also read articles from previous weeks. Updated twice a month.

5

5.2
Air Information/Reservations   **FLIGHTS**

Air Information/Reservations contains the Official Airline Guide Electronic Edition and Travelshopper. Both offer complete schedule and fare information for all commercial flights throughout the world. When using either of these products, you will be asked for your departure and destination cities and your date of travel. Both offer reservations and ticketing options.

5.2.1
OAG Electronic Edition   **OAG**

The Official Airline Guide Electronic Edition contains the schedules and availability for all commercial flights operating throughout the world. It contains fares for all North American and international flights. You can make reservations online and, depending on the airline, can select from several available ticketing options. Information on hotels and motels throughout the world is now available. Updated continually. **$**.

5.2.2
Travelshopper   TWA
Travelshopper gives direct access to the PARS reservation system. You can look up flight availability and fares for any airline in the world. It will select flights that are closest to the travel date and time that you specify. You can make reservations online. Actual ticketing must be done through your travel agent or local airlines. Additional services and travel information are provided in Travelshopper such as weather, theater information, ski conditions and in-flight meals and movies. Updated continually.

5.3
Hotel Information   HOTELS
This section contains information on accommodations for the traveler.

5.3.1
ABC Worldwide Hotel Guide   ABC
The hotel guide provides up-to-date comprehensive listings of over 28,000 hotel properties world wide including location, local and toll-free telephone numbers, credit cards accepted, rates and facilities. You can search for hotels by city, hotel name, chain, rates, special services or amenities. Updated every two months.

5.3.2
OAG Electronic Edition   OAG
Refer to 5.2.1

5.3.3
SUN 'N SAND VACATIONS   SNS
SUN 'N SAND VACATIONS enables you to put together a complete travel package. You can choose from cruises and travel packages to Mexico, the Bahamas, or the Caribbean. There are several different travel agencies offering package tours as well as separate services. Specials are available. The Cruise Shop is an online connection to several of America's most popular cruise lines. Reservations and inquiries may be submitted online. Updated weekly.

5.3.4
American Express® ADVANCE   AXP
American Express® Advance offers a series of online services including financial management programs for individual cardmembers and corporations. Examples of their services include account balance information and travel expense records. Travel services include information and reservations for tours and vacations around the world. Shopping services are also available.

5.3.5
Worldwide Property Guide   **WWX**

Worldwide Exchange is a clearinghouse for the renting, chartering, exchanging or sale of vacation property including vacation homes, condos, RV's and yachts. It also lists bed and breakfast inns throughout the world. Some listings are true bargains while others are the height of luxury. Updated twice a week.

5.4
TravelVision   **TRV**

TravelVision provides information and services that enable you to plan your motor vehicle travel. This section has many products for sale that may be ordered online including road maps and atlases, a routing service for North America, auto tape tours, globes and travel guides. Updated weekly.

5.5
Tours and Cruises   **TRA-7**

This section contains information on travel packages.

5.5.1
SUN 'N SAND VACATIONS   **SNS**

Refer to 5.3.3

5.5.2
American Express® ADVANCE   **AXP**
Refer to 5.3.4

5.6
U.S. Domestic Information   **TRA-8**
This section contains information on travel within the United States.

5.6.1
West Coast Travel   **WESTCOAST**
West Coast Travel is a travel guide by Lee Foster which alerts you to the many pleasures
of travel destinations in the western United States. For each area, Lee describes the flavor,
how to get there, the area's history, the main attractions, nearby trips and where to get
more information. He also has a section featuring articles on special interest travel. Questions may be left for Lee which he will answer in future columns. Updated weekly.

5.6.2
Discover Orlando   **ORLANDO**
Discover Orlando provides current information on hotels/motels, recreation, restaurants and
central Florida attractions such as Walt Disney World, Sea World, Kennedy Space Center,
Circus World, Busch Gardens, Cypress Gardens, Weeki Wachee, Silver Springs and many
more. There are Vacation Special Discounts for CompuServe subscribers. An online reservations and inquiries section is available to assist you in making your Florida vacation
plans. Updated weekly.

5.6.3
Rocky Mountain Connections   **ROCKIES**
Rocky Mountain Connections contains information for vacationing in the Rocky Mountain
States including state attractions, recreation areas, dining, entertainment, accommoda-
tions, ski resorts, and even weather and road conditions. Summer and winter vacation
packages may be reserved online for skiing and other vacation activities. Updated weekly.

5.6.4
Information USA   **INFOUSA**
Information USA tells you how to use the free or nearly free government publications and
services that are available. It explains the art of obtaining information from bureaucrats
and gives other helpful information when dealing with the government. Information USA
was extracted from the reference book of the same name written by Matthew Lesko.

5.6.4.12
Electronic Answer Man   EAM

Do you want to study overseas? How do you patent your invention? Are pests destroying your organic garden? The Electronic Answer Man can help you on almost any topic. EAM describes government publications, public agency departments, and funding sources.

5.7
International Information   TRA-9

This section contains information on international travel.

5.7.1
VISA Advisors   VISA

VISA Advisors is a passport and visa expediting firm located in Washington D.C. providing visa and passport requirements and documents. They will assist you in visa processing, passport processing, and legalization of documents. They charge a service fee per document and hand carry your documents to the embassies or consulates involved. Updated monthly.

5

5.7.3
Dept. of State Advisories   STATE

The United States Department of State's Citizen Emergency Center maintains a continuously updated information service for Americans traveling abroad. Their advisories and warnings cover such conditions as warfare, political unrest, hotel/motel shortages, currency regulations and other information of interest to the American traveler. Updated weekly.

5.7.4
Information USA/International   IUS-1552

Whether you are planning a two-week vacation or an extended residency in a foreign country, the U.S. Government has information that you could use. Lists of American Embassies and consulates, potential health hazards and passport information are available from the State Department. Travelers could also benefit from booklets on cost of living overseas, customs, language materials and foreign schools and hospitals. Information USA will give you names of publications and the agency addresses to obtain them.

5.8
Travel Potpourri   TRA-10

This section contains a variety of travel products.

5.8.1
Worldwide Property Guide   **WWX**
Refer to 5.3.5

5.8.3
Adventures in Travel   **AIT**
Refer to 5.1.6

5.8.5
Information USA   **INFOUSA**
Refer to 5.6.4

5.8.5.12
Electronic Answer Man   **EAM**
Refer to 5.6.4.12

5.9
Travel Forums   **TRA-11**
Do you want to go where the sun keeps shining, the sights are spectacular, or natives are delightful? Then visit one of the travel forums to exchange ideas with fellow travelers.

5.9.1
Travel Forum   **TRAVSIG**
The Travel Forum allows those interested in travel to swap stories, ideas, and information with other forum members. You can talk with others who have already been to your destination to find out the best (or worst) restaurants and hotels. You can learn about the customs in foreign countries and other important information. You can also find out about destination spots and cruises. Leave questions for others or share your experiences.

5.9.2
Florida Forum   **FLORIDA**
The Florida Forum allows residents, vacationers or anyone with an interest in Florida to share information about the sunshine state. You can talk with the residents to find out the best places to stay, eat, or visit if you're planning a vacation. Find information on sporting and recreational activities in the Florida state or events/attractions of interest. A Travel and Trivia Contest is held every week in the forum and guest speakers appear often in the online conferences.

5

5.10
Aviation   AVIATION
This section includes material on flight planning, weather briefing, airport reviews and safety tips.

5.10.1
Aviation Safety Institute   ASI
Aviation Safety Institute provides information on a variety of safety-related topics. Topics include Service Difficulty Reports and Hazard Reports, along with articles on flight operations, human factors, airport reviews and safety tips. The information in ASI Monitor, an online newsletter, is updated monthly.

5.10.2
Aviation Weather   AWX
CompuServe Aviation Weather is instant weather for pilots. It uses the N.O.A.A. Service "A" weather wire. This is the same data used in International Flight Service stations. Most of the data is coded but is easy to read with a little practice. It includes hourly reports, terminal forecasts, NOTAMS, PIREPS, SIGMETS, AIRMETS, area forecasts and radar summaries. Updated continuously. **$**

5.10.3
EMI Aviation Services   EMI

Each of the EMI Aerodata flight planning programs produces a complete flight log for flights between any two points in the continental U.S. in a form suitable for en route navigation. EMI makes available weather briefing, trip time and distance, and a radar map.
For radar weather you need a screen that is at least 80 characters wide. **$**

5.10.4
Aviation Forum (AVSIG)   AVSIG

The Aviation Special Interest Forum is a group of people interested in computers and airplanes. It covers general flying issues, safety, weather, air traffic control, balloons and soaring, want ads and personal computer programs. AVSIG is open to any and all who care to visit and share their ideas and experience in the field of aviation.

5.10.5
Air Information/Reservations   FLIGHTS
Refer to 5.2

5.10.5.1
OAG Electronic Edition   OAG
Refer to 5.2.1

5.10.5.2
Travelshopper   TWA
Refer to 5.2.2

5.10.6
VIDTEX Weather Maps   MAPS

These weather maps can be displayed on most computers running CompuServe's VIDTEX terminal software or using one of the free public-domain graphics decoders from the Aviation Forum. They include a national map, surface synoptic map, and an aviation weather depiction chart. These maps are black and white only. **$**

5.10.8
ModelNet   MODELNET

The Model Aviation Forum is a forum for the model hobbyist. Builders of model railroads, airplanes, cars and boats will find all these disciplines covered in the forum. In addition, forum members have access to newsletters and articles from "Model Aviation Magazine" and a complete contest calendar. A "Swap Shop" enables hobbyists to trade parts.

This chapter contains the CompuServe products that enable you to shop in the comfort of your own home. Depending on the merchant, you can order from online catalogs or have print catalogs sent to your home and order via electronic order forms, by conventional mail or telephone.

6.1
The Electronic MALL®   EM

The Electronic Mall enables you to order products from close to a hundred national retailers without searching for a parking space or waiting in check-out lines. Using your terminal you can order products, use your credit card to pay for them and have them shipped to your home or office. The Electronic Mall is open 24 hours a day, seven days a week and there are no yearly membership fees or surcharges.

The merchants are grouped in mall departments such as Auto, Books/Periodicals, and Financial. Each merchant brings his best products and services to CompuServe subscribers, often at substantial savings. Many offer free catalogs so that you can also order from the merchant using conventional mail or telephone.

The Electronic Mall is growing and changing. In this Almanac we have listed by category the merchants who were in the Mall at time of publication. Please consult the online directory for the list of current merchants. This Week's Mall News (go EMN) announces new merchants and special sales and promotions. You can contact the manufacturers directly through EasyPlex for catalogs or more product information.

6

6.1.1
Shop by Department   EM-4

The merchant directory is displayed by department, along with a brief description and GO code. In this Almanac we have listed by category the merchants who were in the Mall at the time of publication. Please consult the online directory for the list of current merchants.

6.1.1.1
Apparel/Accessories   EM-9

6.1.1.1.1
Apparel Concepts For Men   APC

Apparel Concepts For Men is a North Carolina retailer which offers a distinctive collection of quality menswear, backed by personal service, at very competitive prices. Among the brand names carried are: Hart Schaffner & Mark, Palm Beach, Corbin, London Fog, Gant, Arrow, Gitman Bros., Levi, Lee and Jockey. Also available is a special order shoe service from eight major manufacturers.

6.1.1.1.2
Inside * Outside Lingerie   IO
Browse through a fantasy collection of intimate apparel and gifts. Both men and women can choose lingerie, accessories and at-homewear in silk, satin and cottons. All items are packaged in their own gift box with card enclosure.

6.1.1.1.4
Milkins Jewelers   MJ
Now in their 82nd year, Milkins offers you a wide selection of diamonds, colored stones, pearls, gold jewelry, watches, sterling silver and unique gift suggestions.

6.1.1.2
Auto   EM-11

6.1.1.2.1
AutoVision   **AV**

Today's smart shopper compares products, prices and options at AutoVision. AV's Money Management advice can help you decide whether to buy or lease your next car. Prices of auto makes, models, and options can be compared and new cars can be ordered, financed and delivered through AutoVision. Crevier Leasing Co. and Crevier Motors, Inc. present the modern way to shop for horseless carriages.

6.1.1.2.2
Buick Magazine   **BU**

Buick Magazine offers Buick novelty items, driving tips, and product information in their Mall store. Receive a free gift for answering Buick's online questionnaire.

6.1.1.2.3
Chevy Showroom   **CHV**

Whether you're looking for a part for your '57 Chevy or selecting a new model, the Chevy Showroom can help. Through the great Chevy Swap Meet, you can advertise vehicles and parts "wanted" or "for sale" and exchange information. The Vehicle Recommendation Service surveys your needs and recommends models. You can access information on the latest model lineup, options, and suggested prices. And you can learn about upcoming motor races, investigate auto financing and shop the Chevy Shopper for exciting Chevy products.

6.1.1.2.4
Dutchess CompuLease   **DU**

Dutchess CompuLease is an alternative to the automobile marketplace. With Dutchess CompuLease there is no need for down payments and no need to go through dealer shopping. From the comfort of your own home, you can pick the auto of your choice, and let Dutchess CompuLease do the rest. An online credit application is available. Leasing may be the best way for you to drive that new car you want.

6.1.1.2.5
Ford Motor Company   **FMC**

The Ford Motor Company Electronic Showroom gives you the latest product news and information on automotive subjects and information on Ford's product lineup, manufacturers' suggested retail prices and optional equipment. The Electronic Showroom can help you locate the dealer nearest you and select the car or truck that best suits your needs.

6.1.1.3
Books/Periodicals   EM-12

6.1.1.3.1
Ballantine Books   BAL
Armchair adventurers, look no further. The worlds of mystery, science fiction, humor and best sellers are at your fingertips. Non-fiction, business and reference books are also available for those who take life seriously.

6.1.1.3.2
Dow Jones & Co.   DJ
This prestigious company offers business publications online, including *The Wall Street Journal*, *Barrons* and *National Business Employment Weekly*.

6.1.1.3.3
The McGraw-Hill Book Company   MH
Computer books, video tapes and software. Business, legal and engineering books. Fiction and nonfiction titles from a leading New York trade and business publisher.

6.1.1.3.4
Mercury House   MER
Fiction and nonfiction titles from a California-based publisher.

6.1.1.3.5
Small Computer Book Club   BK
Finally — a book club devoted to books on computers! If you join the Small Computer Book Club you will receive a free book, *How to Get the Most Out of CompuServe*. You can also choose an outstanding set of books for a low introductory price. Each set brings you the latest tools, techniques, and ideas so you can get the most out of your personal computer. And best of all, you save up to 95% off the publisher's price.

6.1.1.3.6
Waldenbooks   WB
The nation's largest bookstore chain offers fiction, nonfiction, and science fiction titles among others. Children's books, computer software, audio and video tapes, games and bargain books are also offered.

6.1.1.4
Computing   **EM-14**

6

6.1.1.4.1
Aaxion Tech Network   **ATN**
The Aaxion Tech Network is a store for big kids that enjoy high tech toys. The Aaxion personal computer product catalog includes software books, computers, office supplies and custom-made vinyl dust covers for computer equipment.

6.1.1.4.2
Computer Express   **CE**
Computer Express carries a full line of Apple, Amiga, IBM, and Macintosh software, as well as hardware for the Apple, IBM and Macintosh, and a special order section to get information on products not online. There's also a toll-free number to find out about discount prices on special orders.

6.1.1.4.3
The Heath Company   **HTH**
Heath Company offers kitbuilding in 16 major categories, including amateur radio, clocks, stereo and weather. Available through Heath is a complete line of Heath/Zenith computers. There is also a Heathkit Electronic Center Location section, to find the Heath store nearest you. For complete descriptions, specifications and photos on all items, you can order Heathkit Catalogs online.

6.1.1.4.4
IBM Canada, Ltd.   IBM

Through IBM Canada Ltd., Canadian subscribers can request free information on many IBM products and services available in Canada. Product information includes PCs, printers, software, computer services, educational services and supplies.

6.1.1.4.6
Investment Software   IS

Investment software is the next best thing to having an investment consultant at your fingertips. Primarily for IBM PCs, the available software covers technical analysis, portfolio management, options, bonds, commodities, real estate/taxes and games/simulations.

6.1.1.4.7
MaryMac Industries Inc.   MM

This authorized Radio Shack dealer is a pioneer in mail-order computers and peripherals. Marymac offers computers and computer products by Tandy, and Epson printers, as well as low discount prices.

6.1.1.4.8
Menu International   MNU

Menu is the international software database information and ordering service for any computer software, for any system — Apple to Zilog, for any subject — Astronomy to Zoology. If you can't decide among the hundreds of software choices, a printed report describing the software that meets your requirements can be produced.

6.1.1.4.9
SAFEWARE Insurance   SAF

Your computer may be your biggest investment after your home and car, and it makes sense to insure it. Vulnerable to theft, power surges and coffee spills, expensive hardware and software is usually not completely covered by traditional insurance.

SAFEWARE is an independent insurance agency that specializes in coverage for high-tech electronic equipment including hardware, software and media. Special coverage is available for overseas locations, rental equipment and high-value systems.

6.1.1.4.11
Software Discounters   SDA

Software Discounters provides you with competitive pricing on software for Commodore, Atari, IBM, Apple and Macintosh personal computers. For the absolute best prices anywhere in software, browse and join their Discount Disk Club, where members are offered a monthly changing list of values.

6.1.1.4.12
CDA Computer Sales   **CDA**
CDA Computer Sales has become one of America's largest mail-order companies be-
cause of its prompt shipping, excellent prices, knowledgeable sales people and technical
support lines. In addition, CDA has a unique, 30-day money-back satisfaction guarantee.
Its catalog features PCs, printers and other accessories.

6.1.1.5
Financial   **EM-17**

6.1.1.5.3
Business Incorporating Guide   **INC**
If you're considering incorporating a business, the Business Incorporating Guide can help
by providing up- to-date information about incorporating anywhere in the United States
and an online order form. Corporate Agents, Inc., a nationwide incorporating service,
sponsors the Business Incorporating Guide.

6.1.1.5.5
Dean Witter Reynolds   **DWR**
Dean Witter Reynolds provides investment and financial services to corporate, institutional
and individual investors in the U.S. and overseas. Test your knowledge through a variety of
on-line quizzes. Learn about the future cost of college education and retirement, and how
to plan for them. Investors can request Dean Witter's Recommended List, the only publicly
audited stock recommendations on the Street. Have your investment questions answered
by a Dean Witter Account Executive through the Open Line for Your Questions. Free brochures are available to help you plan your financial future.

6.1.1.5.7
First Texas Savings   **FT**
Texas is one of the most competitive financial markets in the nation. As a result, First Texas
Savings pays you high interest rates on savings and investments. Established in 1890,
First Texas Savings is a full service financial institution. Telebanking representatives are
available electronically or by toll-free telephone to answer questions or help you set up the
IRA, CD or Money Market accounts that are best for you.

6.1.1.5.8
H&R Block HRB

H&R Block is the world's largest income tax service, preparing one out of every 10 individual income tax returns in the United States. You can learn about Block's history and the many services provided, including Tax Forecaster, a written analysis of how the new tax laws affect you, and Rapid Refund, Block's electronic filing program. Also included are answers to tax questions, tax saving tips, and a comprehensive list of changes brought about by the Tax Reform Act of 1986.

6.1.1.5.9
Max Ule Discount Brokerage MU

Information on online brokerage services, including Tickertec, the real time market monitoring system for home and office, and Tickerscreen, a service that allows PC owners to buy and sell stocks and bonds at discount prices and obtain daily closing quotes.

6.1.1.6
Gifts/Novelties EM-19

6.1.1.6.2
Executive Stamper EX

Give a unique and personal gift to that special person. Choose from a catalog of gifts and type styles from Executive Stamper. Items range from plaques, trophies, and baseball caps to brass card cases, office door signs, and rubber stamps.

6.1.1.6.3
Hawaiian Isle   **HI**

A unique selection of Hawaiian products, including floral arrangements, tropical plants, Hawaiian gourmet treats, fragrances, books, clothing and gifts. Information on Hawaiian Isle Adventure is also available upon request.

6.1.1.6.4
Lincoln Manor Baskets   **LM**

Individualized baskets are a simple, elegant expression of gratitude, celebration or thoughtfulness. Each basket is individually designed and assembled from the finest products: Crabtree & Evelyn bath and food products, fine chocolates, gourmet foods and unique gift items. Baskets are available for new babies, get well wishes, congratulations and to say thank you. Seasonal holiday baskets are also available.

6.1.1.6.5
Tooth Fairyland   **TF**

Yes, the Tooth Fairy has entered the electronic age. Commemorate that once-in-a-lifetime moment of loosing that first tooth by making it official. The First Tooth Loss Gift Package includes a certificate from the Tooth Fairy Documentation Center, an official Tooth Fairy Lost Tooth Alert Light and a T-shirt that proclaims, "I just lost my first tooth".

6.1.1.7
Gourmet/Flowers   **EM-20**

6.1.1.7.1
Coffee Emporium   **COF**

A family owned and operated old-fashioned coffeehouse is as close as your keyboard. The Coffee Emporium, located in the San Francisco Bay area, promptly fills orders using the highest grade gourmet coffee beans, Arabica AA & A. In addition, Coffee Emporium carries a complete line of gourmet teas, coffee samplers and coffee and tea making accessories.

6.1.1.7.2
Fifth Avenue Shopper   **FTH**

Flowers for all occasions and gift baskets of fruit, all delivered by leading wire services.

6

6.1.1.7.3
Florida Fruit Shippers   **FFS**

Fresh Florida grapefruit, oranges, citrus, pineapples, and avocados are available. Discover gourmet Florida seafood, including giant stone crab claws and lobster tails. Jams, jellies, as well as gourmet gift packages are provided.

6.1.1.7.4
Simon David   **SIM**

This Dallas-based gourmet food shop brings you the best in delicacies and gift items. Their catalog features specialty meats (including rattlesnake meat!), smoked meats, fresh fruits, candies, and nuts. A wide selection of gift packs, including a Texas Gift Box, are also offered.

6.1.1.7.5
Walter Knoll Florist   **WK**

If you forgot someone's birthday or just want to say "thanks", flowers can deliver your message, usually within 24 hours. Walter Knoll offers a wide selection of arrangements including holiday bouquets, bud vases, corsages, fruit and flower baskets, planters, balloon bouquets and special orders just for you.

6.1.1.8
Health/Beauty   **E-29**

6.1.1.8.1
B&K Beauty Supplies   **BS**

B & K Beauty Supplies, a professional hair care center, carries a large selection of retail professional care products for hair, skin, nails and bath. You can choose from high quality name brands such as Paul Mitchell, Redken, Nexxus, Sebastian International and Aveda. If your favorite professional brand is not listed, B & K Beauty Supplies will find it for you. You can order online or send for their complete catalog of beauty products.

6.1.1.9
Hobbies/Toys   **EM-22**

6.1.1.9.1
Hobby Center Toys   **HC**

Good news for kids of all ages! Hobby Center Toys has an exciting collection of toys, games, stuffed animals and pre-school delights. Hobby items such as model trains, kits and radar control toys are also available.

6.1.1.9.2
TSR Hobby Shop   **TSR**

Fans of adventure games can stop their searching because TSR Hobby Shop has what you need. Discover rules, accessories and books on Dungeons & Dragons® and other simulation games. Adventure novels, science fiction games and miniatures are also offered.

6.1.1.10
Home/Appliance   **EM-21**

6.1.1.10.1
Black & Decker Powerline Network   **BD**

Shop for Black & Decker power tools at the new Black & Decker Powerline Network. You will find a wide variety of quality power tools for your auto, garden, work shop and hobby projects. The Powerline Network is an independent Black & Decker distributor that offers many exclusive items to CompuServe subscribers. The Super Discount Special of the Month offers fantastic savings.

6

6.1.1.11
Merchandise/Electronics   **EM-23**

6.1.1.11.1
AT&T   **ATT**

AT&T Search has three parts. Search Central gives an online catalog of telephone and answering systems, computers, long distance services and do-it-yourself accessories. Search Guides offers personalized assistance in choosing the products and services that best suit your needs. And Search Contest is a monthly challenge providing fun and prizes.

6.1.1.11.2
CompuServe Store　　　　　　　　　　**ORDER**

The CompuServe Store is the ordering service for CompuServe products. Order the CompuServe Almanac, users guides, software, posters, books, T-shirts, and more. Make the best use of your connect time by knowing what CompuServe offers and how to use it.

6.1.1.11.3
Crutchfield　　　　　　　　　　　　　**CFD**

Request a free copy of the renowned Crutchfield catalog of high quality, name-brand consumer electronics including audio/visual equipment, telephones, security products, car stereos and more. All products come with a 30-day guarantee.

6.1.1.11.4
Garden Camera & Electronics　　　　　**GC**

Visit Garden Camera & Electronics for the latest in consumer electronics and photography equipment. From the heart of Manhattan's camera & electronics district come name-brand products such as Panasonic, Sony, JVC, Nikon, Canon, Minolta, Whistler, Bel and Olympus. You can save even more during monthly specials.

6.1.1.11.6
Stereo/Video Factory　　　　　　　　　**SV**

Tune into the Stereo/Video Factory for good buys on entertainment equipment. You can shop their selection of video cassette recorders (VCRs), color televisions, video camcorders, and stereo equipment for home or car. On the message line you can special order equipment or ask questions, such as whether a stereo or speakers can be installed in your car. The Stereo/Video Factory's low prices include shipping to anywhere in the country.

6.1.1.12
Music/Movies   EM-28

6.1.1.12.1
Express Music   EMC
Rock, jazz, classical and country compact discs. Their catalog features over 21,000 titles.

6.1.1.12.2
Magic Castle Video   MV
A full service video store that carries video equipment including laser disc players and extensive online catalogs of videotapes and laser discs.

6.1.1.12.3
Music Alley Online   MAO
For your instrumental needs, whether you need a guitar or a sound effects machine, mixers, amplifiers, or bass amplifier, Music Alley Online can help. Music Alley Online offers pre- and post-sales advice and help, as well as a special order service.

6.1.1.12.4
BMG Direct Marketing, Inc.   BMG
Formerly a service of RCA Direct Marketing, BMG Direct Marketing, Inc. offers a Compact Disc Club, with a free disc when you join, a Video Club, a Music Service Club, and the International Preview Society, a classical music club. All four clubs offer savings off suggested retail prices.

6.1.1.13
Office Supplies   EM-40

6.1.1.13.1
Great Lakes Business Forms   GL
While some companies sell business forms as a sideline, Great Lakes Business Forms specializes in stock forms for the commercial, financial and industrial communities. All items offered online are packaged in small quantities, and most products are priced under $15.00 to fit home budgets.

6

6.1.1.13.2
Office Machines & Supplies   OM

Office Machines & Supplies Co. sells and services IBM and AT&T, Royal, Olivetti, and Sharm office equipment. Their inventory includes typewriters, ribbons, supplies, computers, printers and copiers.

6.1.1.14
Online Services   EM-25

6.1.1.14.1
EF Hutton   EF

Huttonline turns your personal computer into a powerful investment tool. Timely account data and news are at your fingertips. You can monitor your account, the stock market, and the world of investments. And with Huttonline's electronic mail service, you can eliminate "telephone tag" with your stock broker. Request a Huttonline brochure online.

6.1.1.14.2
NewsNet   NN

NewsNet is the largest online database of specialized business publications. You save time and money, and keep on top of your field, with this quick one stop news service. NewsNet monitors hundreds of publications and newsletters for you. Keyword searching and automatic retrieval of articles provide you with customized business news.

6.1.1.14.3
Official Airline Guides   OA

Official Airline Guides offers information on the OAG Electronic Edition, the unbiased flight and fare system for today's traveler. The OAG Electronic Edition contains direct and connecting flight schedules of every scheduled airline worldwide, plus fares for North American flights. The OAG Electronic Edition can be accessed by typing GO OAG. Travel guides including the pocket flight guides and travel planner are available for purchase.

6.1.1.15
Premium Merchants   EM-27

6.1.1.15.1
American Express®   **AXM**

The American Express® Merchandise shop features a wide selection of electronics, robots, games, travel items, and health and fitness products. Cookbooks and magazines are also offered. Free print catalog.

6.1.1.15.3
Neiman-Marcus   **NM**

Neiman-Marcus is synonymous with distinctive merchandise of the finest quality. Open a Neiman-Marcus charge account, order a print catalog or order from the print catalog.

6.1.1.16
Sports/Leisure   **EM-30**

6.1.1.16.1
Air France   **AF**

Information on flights and packages to Paris, the Riviera, and other parts of France. Travel tips and tours. Video cassette lending library. Free travel brochures.

6

6.1.1.16.2
Ameropa Travel   **AT**

Travel to London, Paris, Rome, Frankfort, Amsterdam, Brussels, Milan, Geneva, Zurich or Munich from more than 20 gateways within the United States on full-service flights at super low fares. Flexible options include one-way or round-trip reservations, or flying into one city and returning from another. Check schedules and make reservations the easy way.

6.1.1.16.3
Bike Barn   **BB**

If you are dreaming of two-wheeled fun, pull into the Bike Barn. You can browse through their inventory of bicycles, bicycle parts, accessories and apparel for the whole family. The Bike Barn carries Panasonic bicycles for men and women: beach cruisers, 3-speeds, sport/touring 10-speeds, racers and mountain bikes. Starter and BMX bikes are available for youngsters. The well-dressed cyclist can choose shorts, jerseys, helmets and many accessories from the Bike Barn. Keep in shape even if the snow flies! Windtrainers and exercise bicycles can keep you pedalling all winter.

6.1.1.16.5
Ryn Robin Pool & Patio   **RR**

Everything you ever needed for your pool, patio or spa. Ryn Robin's catalog includes pool maintenance products, water games, hot tub items, books, outdoor and beach chairs, hammocks, rubber duckies — even a floating island raft.

6.1.2
Shop by Merchant   **EM-8**

The merchant directory is displayed either alphabetically or by department, along with a brief description and Quick Reference Word. In this Almanac we have listed by category the merchants who were in the Mall at the time of publication. Please consult the online directory for the list of current mall merchants.

6.1.3
Index to Products   **INX**

The product index lists by category merchandise found in the Mall.

6.1.4
Electronic Mall News   **EMN**

The Electronic Mall News enables the smart shopper to keep up with the latest happenings in the Mall. Special offers, contests and their results, new products and merchants are featured every week.

6.1.5
How to Shop at the Mall   EM-6
This section describes the Electronic Mall, tells how to order products, outlines payment options, gives price information, tells how to check the status of an order and offers helpful hints.

6.1.6
Talk to the Mall Manager   EM-7
If you have questions or problems with a specific merchant or suggestions on how to improve the mall, you can leave a message for the mall manager. The manager will respond to you via EasyPlex.

6.2
Comp-u-store Online   CUS
Now you can join the thousands of other educated consumers who access America's largest discount electronic shopping service. Shop at home for more than 250,000 name-brand products — with savings of up to 50 percent.

Now you can access Comp-u-store OnLine as a CompuServe subscriber and browse through the electronic database for everything from air conditioners to computers to microwaves. Comp-u-store OnLine is your link to major manufacturers, wholesalers, and suppliers. That means that as a member you pay much less since costly retail price mark-ups, inventories and storefronts are eliminated. When you decide to buy, your low price includes delivery right to your door. There are no hidden costs. Your purchase comes in a factory-sealed carton with all manufacturer's warranties and guarantees in full effect.

The Comp-u-store OnLine shopping service does not end with the 250,000 product selection. While OnLine, visit Comp-u-mall — a collection of fine specialty shops offering something for everyone. Select fine foods from our Gourmet Food Shops, including Omaha Steaks, Hickory Farms and Double Truffle Chocolates. Looking for a special gift? Long Distant Roses, The E.A. Carey Smokeshop, Stanley Tools and 800 Spirits are just a few of the national retailers located in Comp-u-mall.

Comp-u-store OnLine's Auctions and Amusements offer you ways to have fun while saving money. Use your computer skills to solve our Scavenger Hunt and win valuable prizes. Participate in the weekly auctions to bid against other members across the U.S. and save hundreds of dollars on such items as TV's, VCR's, stereo equipment, sports equipment and more.

Comp-u-store OnLine's Consumer and Customer Service Areas were created with you in mind. Consumer Services include Classified Ads, Software Reviews, The Consumer Hotline and ERA Real Estate. The Information Booth, our Customer Service Center, is where you can send questions or offer suggestions. Learn about membership bonuses such as the free VISA card and Comp-u-bucks.

Visit Comp-u-store OnLine today, and you'll have a world of savings at your fingertips. The CompuServe Users Guide shows you how.

6

6.3
CompuServe's SOFTEX^{SM} Software Catalog   **SOFTEX**

CompuServe's SOFTEX^{SM} is an electronic software catalog which enables you to purchase and receive commercial software through your personal computer without the inconvenience of driving to a computer store or waiting for mail delivery. SOFTEX's growing selection includes popular commercially-available software as well as hard-to-find software from smaller vendors. Selections include programming utilities, tutorials, spreadsheets, accounting packages and games for most personal computers.

Your machine requires terminal software that supports an error-checking file transfer protocol, such as XMODEM or CompuServe's "B" protocol. Purchases are billed to your CompuServe account.

6.4
Order from CompuServe   **ORDER**

Access CompuServe's online ordering service and place your order selecting from CompuServe's many exciting products — from users guides, T-shirts, game maps, posters and more. You can also check on an existing order's status and change an order before it is filled. You are not charged for connect time viewing descriptions or placing an order. You are, however, charged for communications surcharges.

6.5
New Car Showroom   **NEWCAR**

New Car Showroom is a comparison shopping guide for consumers making new vehicle purchases. You can examine and compare features and specifications of passenger cars, trucks, vans and special-purpose vehicles. Over 700 foreign and domestic cars and trucks are compared in prices, standard and optional features and technical specifications, such as fuel economy and roominess.

6.6
Online Today Online Inquiry   **OLI**

You can request general information about an ad displayed in *Online Today* and request product literature directly from advertisers.

7

This chapter provides information and services to individual investors along with personal finance offerings on such matters as taxes, insurance and financial planning. You can get quotes on stock prices, find out information about companies, buy and sell securities and do home banking. Some products enable you to enter a previously stored file of ticker symbols and obtain quotes for each company in your file. Others will give you information simply by entering the name of the company preceded by an asterisk (i.e. *XEROX).

Symbols used in many of the products can be found in the Appendix.

7.1
Market Quotes/Highlights   QUOTES

This menu delivers CompuServe's MicroQuote II via menus. Experienced subscribers of these services may wish to access this service in command mode (GO MQUOTE).

The MicroQuote database contains current and historical information on more than 90,000 stocks, bonds, mutual funds, and options as well as foreign exchange rates and hundreds of market indexes. Dividend, interest, distribution and split histories go back to 1968 and daily price and volume data are available back to 1974 for selected issues. MicroQuote II also contains investment data on earnings, risk, and capitalization. MicroQuote II current stock quotes are delayed approximately 20 minutes. Most commodities data are available by 6:00 p.m. Eastern Time, and price and volume information for all securities is updated and available by 8:00 a.m. the next morning.

CompuServe is very careful about the accuracy of its MicroQuote II data. We perform automated reasonability tests and use independent sources to check any discrepancies. Many major investment banking firms regularly depend upon this data.

Here are a few tips that you may find useful when using MicroQuote II:

- For stock information you will need to enter a ticker symbol or the first six digits of a CUSIP. If you do not know either of these, you can look them up using the Issue/Symbol Lookup programs, GO SYMBOLS.

- If you are at a prompt for company name or ticker symbol and you wish to exit the program, the navigational commands such as TOP or MENU will not work. Instead you need to enter /T or /M so that the system knows you are not trying to enter a company name or ticker symbol.

- For some products you will need to enter the date or the number of days, weeks or months for which you wish pricing information. Dates may be entered in several formats including mm/dd/yy (i.e. 10/15/87 or 2/7/86).

- Codes for popular Mutual funds, market indicators, stocks, exchange rates and commodities are listed in the Appendix.

7.1.1
Current Quotes   **QQUOTE**

Quick Quote, CompuServe's current quotations service includes information from national and regional exchanges and the OTC national market on over 9,000 stocks. Quotes are delayed 20 minutes, which is as soon as the exchanges will allow you to receive them without the payment of a monthly fee. The information includes volume, high, low, last, change and time of last trade or quote.

You can retrieve the quotes by specifying a ticker symbol, CUSIP, the company name or a previously stored file of ticker symbols. Optionally, retrieved data may be directed to an output file in formats readable by microcomputer spreadsheet packages. See Appendixes D and F for lists of symbols used in this product.

Updated continually. **$**

7.1.2
Historical Stock/Fund Pricing   **SECURITIES**

This menu accesses the historical part of the MicroQuote II database in a variety of ways.

7.1.2.1
Pricing History — 1 Issue   **PRICES**

Pricing History — 1 Issue gives historical prices by day, week or month. It includes CUSIP, exchange code, volume, high/ask, low/bid and close/average for a given security. You may designate the beginning and ending date or a number of time periods prior to the most recent quote. See Appendixes D, E, F, G and H for lists of symbols used in this product.

Updated daily. **$**

7.1.2.2
Multiple Issues — 1 Day   **QSHEET**

Multiple Issues — 1 Day gives volume, close/average, high/ask, low/bid and CUSIP numbers for several issues for a given day. You may enter a previously stored file of up to 500 ticker symbols for processing. See Appendixes D, E, F, G and H for lists of symbols used in this product. **$**

    Updated daily. **$**

7.1.2.3
Price/Volume Graph   **TREND**

Price/Volume charting provides graphic presentations of both the traded price and the trading volume for the requested days, weeks, or months. Relevant information such as the current earnings, price, dividend, and risk information for common stocks and other securities is displayed with the graph. The program works with CompuServe's VIDTEX software or NAPLPS hardware. Your personal computer must be able to support graphics to use this product. See Appendixes D, E, F, G and H for lists of symbols used in this product. **$**

7.1.2.4
Dividends, Splits, Bond Interest   **DIVIDENDS**

Dividends, Splits, Bond Interest gives dividend, split and bond interest information for an issue over a given period. Hard-to-obtain mutual fund distributions are also available. You may specify the number of dividends you wish to view. The report includes the ex-date, record date, payment date, distribution type and the rate or amount of each distribution. See Appendixes D and F for lists of symbols used in this product.

    Updated daily. **$**

7

7.1.2.5
Pricing Statistics   **PRISTATS**

Pricing History Summarized provides a snapshot of price and volume performance for a requested issue over a given period. It indicates such items as whether an issue is trading closer to recent high or low prices. The statistics include the current high/ask, low/bid, and close average as well as the highest high, the highest close, the lowest low, the lowest close, the highest volume, the lowest volume, and the average and standard deviation for high, low, close, and volume. Also included are the total volume, the beta factor and the beta centile rank. See Appendixes D, E, F, G and H for lists of symbols used in this product.

    Updated daily. **$**

7.1.2.6
Detailed Issue Examination　　　　　　　　　　**EXAMINE**

Detailed Issue Examination gives a detailed description of a single issue including trading status, recent price, dividends, risk measures and capitalization. For stocks, it shows the shares outstanding, twelve-month earnings-per-share, beta factor, indicated annual dividend, and the dividend yield. For bonds, the program includes the maturity date, bond rate, yield to maturity, interest payment history and amount outstanding. Options information includes shares per contract, open interest, expiration date, and exercise price. A 52-week high and low price are included for all securities. See Appendixes D, E, F, G and H for lists of symbols used in this product. **$**

7.1.2.7
Options Profile　　　　　　　　　　　　　　**OPRICE**

Options Profile lists all options currently trading on a given common stock or market index. Coverage includes over 10,000 put and call options trading on major US and Canadian exchanges. It lists the name, closing price, pricing date, ticker symbol and exchange code for the underlying company. The exercise price and closing option price are displayed for each active option. See Appendixes E and F for lists of symbols used in this product.
　　　Updated daily. **$**

7.1.2.8
Instructions/Fees　　　　　　　　　　　　　**MQP**

This section gives instructions on how to use Pricing History (GO PRICES), Multiple Issues (GO QSHEET) and Price/Volume Graph (GO TREND).

7.1.3
Highlights — Previous Day　　　　　　　　　**MARKET**

Market Highlights analyzes the most recent trading day for the New York Stock Exchange, American Stock Exchange, and Over-The-Counter markets and prepares 19 different reports. Included are the most active stocks, the largest gainers and losers, stocks for which the price has risen or dropped over the past three, four, or five trading days, stocks with new 6-month highs or lows, stocks with a low above yesterday's high or a high below yesterday's low, and stocks which have traded twice their average volume. See Appendix F for a list of optionable stocks.
　　　Updated daily. **$**

7.1.4
Commodity Markets   **COMMODITIES**

CompuServe offers access to historical information on commodities futures and cash prices along with exclusive newsletters offering news, features, recommendations and analysis.

CompuServe's commodities database contains open, high, low, settling, and cash prices along with volume and open interest for every trading day since January, 1979. Futures prices are generally available by 6:00 p.m. Eastern time with the cash price, volume, and open interest available 24 hours later. The data is provided by MJK Associates which uses multiple sources to ensure accuracy and guarantee timeliness. Data is available for all commodities on the U.S. or Canadian exchanges with significant trading volume. Data includes financial and currency futures as well as metal, petroleum, and agricultural commodity contracts. Composite prices from Commodity Research Bureau are also available.

A list of Commodity Symbols can be found in Appendix I.

7.1.4.1
Commodity Pricing — One Contract, Many Days   **CPRICE**

Pricing History — One Contract presents historical performance by day, week, or month for the requested delivery period for the requested commodity (or optionally the nearest delivery). The program displays open, high, low, and settling prices along with volume and open interest. Also available are aggregated volume and open interest for all contracts for the requested commodity along with the cash market price for the commodity. A list of commodity symbols can be found in Appendix I.

Updated daily. **$**

7.1.4.2
News-a-tron Market Reports   **NAT**

Market Reports gives analysis and information on petroleum, metals, currency, Foreign Exchange prices, credit markets, domestic and international interest rates, grain reports and current quotes. See Appendixes E, G and H for lists of symbols used in this product. **$**

7.1.4.3
Agri-Commodities, Inc.   **ACI**

Futures Focus is a weekly newsletter for the futures trader published by Agri-Commodities, a leading agricultural and futures consultant to governments and corporations worldwide. It features the TSF trading system, trading recommendations, a market overview and tips on how to improve one's trading performance. Updated weekly. See Appendix E for a list of popular market indicators. **$**

7.1.5
No-Load Mutual Funds   NOLOAD

The No-Load Mutual Fund Association provides extensive information regarding no-load and low-load mutual funds currently available on the market including a one paragraph overview of the fund's objective and its strategy for achieving that objective. Fund information may be retrieved by designating the fund manager, the fund name, the strategy of the fund, the initial investment requirement, and several other criteria. Each fund displays the above information as well as the CompuServe and the NASD ticker symbol, and key features for the fund. Requests for additional information on specific funds can be entered online and will be forwarded to the funds for mail reply. See Appendix D for a list of popular mutual fund symbols.
   Updated monthly.

7.1.6
Investment Analysis   ANALYSIS

Investment Analysis menu selections offer various methods of using MicroQuote II investment data. Disclosure Screening and Securities Screening give subscribers the opportunity to search the entire Disclosure universe of our 9,000 companies or the MicroQuote universe of our 90,000 securities respectively for prospective purchase candidates. Return Analysis and Portfolio Valuation can then be used to track purchased securities and gauge your success.

7.1.6.1
Company Screening   COSCREEN

Company Screening makes it possible to screen the Disclosure II database based on entered criteria and produce a list of companies that meet the criteria. The ticker symbols of the companies can be saved for use in other CompuServe programs. Selection criteria include a variety of growth rates and financial ratios along with SIC codes, state, total assets, book value, market value, annual sales, net income, cash flow, latest price, etc. See Appendix F for a list of optionable stocks.
   Updated weekly with market prices updated daily. $E

7.1.6.2
Securities Screening   SCREEN

This product enables you to enter selected investment criteria and then screen the MicroQuote II database to see what securities meet your criteria. You can search on latest price, exchange, beta, earnings, SIC code or similar criteria. Selection criteria include a variety of growth rates and financial ratios along with SIC codes, state, total assets, book value, market value, annual sales, net income, cash flow, latest stock prices, etc. See Appendixes D, E and F for lists of symbols used in this product.
   Securities Screening is useful for buying into or selling short and for picking bonds with specific maturity dates and yield targets. It is updated weekly with market prices updated daily. $E

7.1.6.3
Return Analysis   **RETURN**

Return Analysis calculates the holding period and annualized returns for as many as 30 requested securities. Symbols specifying the issues may be entered at the terminal or from a stored file. Since the subscriber enters the holding period, this product is useful for analyzing the historical performances of specific issues such as mutual funds in bull and bear markets. See Appendixes D, E, F, G and H for lists of symbols used in this product.
> Updated daily. **$**E

7.1.6.4
Portfolio Valuation   **PORT**

Portfolio Valuation finds the value of a previously created portfolio for dates you select and displays unrealized gains and losses. See Appendixes D, E, F, G and H for lists of symbols used in this product.
> Updated daily. **$**

7.1.7
Issue/Symbol Lookup   **SYMBOLS**

Through this menu you can determine what securities and indexes are included in MicroQuote II and the access symbol for each. Updated daily.

7.1.7.1
Search for Company Name, Ticker Symbol or CUSIP   **CUSIP**

This program will search by name, CUSIP number, or ticker symbol and list all the issues for a company you select. The program displays the ticker symbol, CUSIP number, exchange code and the name and description for each issue. See Appendixes D, E, F, G and H for lists of symbols used in this product. **$**

7.1.7.2
List Bonds for Company   **BONDS**

Bonds Listing displays all active bonds for the designated company. The report includes the ticker symbols, the CUSIP numbers, an issue description, and the yield and the current selling price for each bond. Also included in the report is the quality rating expressed by both Standard & Poor's and Moody's. See Appendix F for a list of optionable stocks.
> Updated daily. **$**

7

7.1.7.3
Menu of Available Indexes   **INDICATORS**

This product gives the ticker and the CUSIP number for all indexes included in the Micro-Quote II database along with the time period for which each index has data. Issues are categorized in manageable groups designated by Market/Industry Indexes, Bonds/Yields, Exchange Rates, Volumes, Advances and Declines, and any issues which are new or do not fall into one of the previous categories. An option is available which lists all indexes without going through the menus. Each index is updated daily.

Lists of Market Indicators, Bond Yield Indicators and Exchange Rate Symbols can be found in Appendixes E, G and H respectively.

7.1.7.4
Menu of Available Commodities   **CSYMBOL**

Commodity Group Listing displays available commodity groups including foods, woods, grains/feeds, fats/oils, metals, financial, petroleum, fibers, currencies and indexes. Access symbols, exchange, and issue description are shown for each commodity. A list of Commodity Symbols can be found in Appendix I.

7.2
Company Information   **COMPANY**

This menu provides access to the various sources of information on specific companies.

7.2.1
Ticker Retrieval   **TICKER**

Ticker Retrieval displays a menu of the information available for the requested company along with the current market quote for the company's common stock. Menu choices direct the subscriber to MicroQuote II, and to Disclosure II, the Institutional Brokers Estimate System, Standard & Poor's, and Value Line, depending on which of these services contain information on the company. Menu choices include price, volume, and dividend history, a statistical analysis of the market performance, descriptive data from Standard & Poor's and Disclosure, projections from Value Line and the Institutional Brokers Estimate System, financial statements from Disclosure and Value Line, and ownership information from Disclosure/SPECTRUM. You may also choose a listing of bonds issued, an option summary and a return analysis program. See Appendix F for a list of optionable stocks. **$**E

7.2.2
OTC NewsAlert   **OTCNEWS**

OTC NewsAlert is a database and clipping service that tracks activities that could affect stock prices of all large and small companies whose stocks trade over-the-counter. Investors, corporate information officers, and competitors can search both recent and historic articles featuring summary earning reports, large sales contracts, new products, acquisitions, takeovers, movements of large blocks of stocks by corporate insiders, and attempts to take companies private. Also included is information on initial public offerings. Information is obtained from a variety of news services, from filings with the Securities and Exchange Commission, and from the companies themselves. OTC NewsAlert items can be searched by company name, stock symbol or topic. A clipping file can be set up through the Executive News Service to follow individual company and industry trends.

7.2.3
Value Line Annual Report   **VLINE**

Value Line Corporate Reports includes information for over 1,700 companies, representing 95% of the dollar value of stocks traded on major U.S. exchanges. Data is provided from 1969 forward where possible.

Value Line Annual Reports are compact financial statements for industrial and service companies. Four annual statements, the balance sheet, income statement, sources and uses of funds, and key ratios report are available.

Value Line Quarterly Reports summarize information for the four quarters in any available fiscal year including sales, EPS, net income, dividend and stock price data. See Appendix F for a list of optionable stocks. **$**

7.2.4
Value Line Quarterly Report   **VLQTR**

7.2.5
S&P's Green Sheets   **S&P**

The Standard & Poor's General Information File contains a business summary, analysis of important developments, product line contributions to profits, corporate officers and selected financial items and future earnings projections for over 3000 companies. Included in this program is the most recent S & P rating. See Appendix F for a list of optionable stocks.

Updated weekly. **$**

7

7.2.6
Disclosure II   **DISCLOSURE**

The Disclosure II database is compiled from the 10K reports that all publicly-owned companies file with the Securities and Exchange Commission. This information includes financial statements and ratios, business segment data, 5-year financial summaries, company name and address, a list of SEC filings, a business description, officers and directors, an ownership and subsidiary summary, and lists of insider owners, institutional owners, and owners of 5% or more of the company's stock. It also includes the management discussion. See Appendix F for a list of optionable stocks.

Updated weekly with market prices updated daily. **$**E

7.3
Banking/Brokerage Services   **BROKERAGE**

This menu enables you to choose among the many banking and brokerage services on CompuServe.

7.3.1
Participating Banks   **BANKING**

Home Banking delivers banking services directly to you through your personal computer or terminal. It is a convenient way for managing your money from your home or office, 24 hours a day, seven days a week.

Home Banking services allow you to view your account balances, pay bills, and transfer funds, and may include information on the latest bank products and services, branch and ATM locations, and current interest rates. Many have the ability to correspond with your banker via electronic mail.

Each of the participating banks offers its customers slightly different banking services. Please check the online description of the banks you are considering for their services and interest rates. Also check the service for new banks in your area since several banks offer electronic banking services on CompuServe.

As of October, 1987 these services were provided by banks servicing Pennsylvania, Florida and Tennessee.

7.3.2
Quick Way   QWK

Quick Way offers all the functions of a traditional stockbroker conveniently through your computer including market and limit orders and trading on margin. The service is provided by Quick & Reilly, a large discount brokerage firm. Buy or sell orders may be placed 24 hours per day with online confirmation when the order is executed. Portfolio evaluation includes value, income, unrealized gains and losses, and year-to-date realized gains and losses. For monthly exchange fees, you can get real-time quotes (otherwise quotes are delayed approximately 20 minutes). **$**

7.3.3
Unified Management   UMC

Unified offers several brokerage services related to the mutual funds which they manage. Advice is offered on retirement plans, financial planning, managed accounts, and mutual funds. UMC offers the Liquid Green Trust and the UNI$SAVE Account which combines a money market account, a checking account and brokerage services and offers expense analysis for 50 categories. Included in the service is a glossary of financial terms which is useful in understanding investment jargon. See Appendix D for a list of popular mutual fund symbols.

   Updated daily.

7.3.4
Max Ule Discount Brokerage   TKR

Max Ule's Tickerscreen conveniently provides nighttime and weekend trading services. Buy and sell orders can be placed for execution and confirmation the next time the market opens. Closing or real-time quotes may be retrieved, and a market summary is included. Additional discount brokerage services include IRA's, money funds, Keoghs, "Ginnie Mae's", etc. The Tickerscreen database also includes unit trust pricing, and Mergersource merger information. Tickertec enables you to track from 48 to 96 different stocks on a real-time basis. You can also purchase Tickertec software. See Appendix D for a list of popular mutual fund symbols.

   Updated daily. **$**

7.4
Earnings/Economic Projections   EARNINGS

This menu choice enables you to access information about different companies earnings, projected earnings and economic projections.

7.4.1
VLINE 3-5 Year Projections   **VLFORE**
Value Line includes estimates for over 1,700 companies representing 95 percent of the dollar value of stocks traded on major U.S. exchanges. Each company forecast projects earnings, sales, dividends, book value, shares outstanding, and high and low prices for from three to five years into the future. Updated quarterly. See Appendix F for a list of optionable stocks. **$**

7.4.2
I/B/E/S Reports   **IBES**
I/B/E/S is the Institutional Broker's Estimate System and represents a consensus of annual and long-term forecasts from more than 2,500 analysts at 130 brokerage and institutional research firms. These firms include the top 20 research firms in the country and 100 percent of the all-star analysts as ranked by the Institutional Investor magazine. The database includes information about more than 3,400 companies and reports the most optimistic and pessimistic EPS estimates as well as median, mean, and variation. Current share price, earnings per share, and price/earnings ratio are included. Updated weekly with market values updated daily. See Appendix F for a list of optionable stocks. **$E**

7.4.4
S&P's Green Sheets   **S&P**
Refer to 7.2.5

7.4.5
MMS Financial Reports   **MMS**
Money Market Services is a multinational corporation specializing in financial and economic research. MMS has expertise in monetary theory and forecasting of central banking policies and operations. They produce a series of economic reports released on a daily, weekly, or monthly basis.

MMS offer several different products on CompuServe including Daily Comment, Fedwatch, Market Briefings, and the Ask Mr. Fed Forum. Surcharges apply only to current reports. See Appendixes G and H for lists of symbols used in this product. **$***

7.4.5.2
Daily Technical Comment   **DC**
Daily Comment explores the technical aspects of market activity and the relationship between the cash and futures market. Support and resistance trends are discussed along with advanced analysis and trading ranges.

7.4.5.3
Fedwatch   **FW**

Fedwatch is a bulletin produced by MMS that focuses on interest rate trends. It is written and released each Thursday afternoon after relevant Federal Reserve data is released (i.e., M1). It focuses on Federal Reserve Board activity and the value of the dollar. **$***

7.4.5.4
Market Briefings   **MAR**

Market Briefings contains various articles written by senior analysts at MMS and is designed to provide an investor with timely, concise analysis of key issues affecting the national debt, stock futures and foreign exchange markets. There are six different reports in Market Briefings including the Quarterly Economic Report, the Forex Report, a schedule of when economic data will be released by the government, a Monetary Outlook Report, a Futures Market Report, and a Treasury Auction Analysis. **$**

The Quarterly Economic Report is a bi-weekly analysis of quarterly GNP and Flow of Funds data. The report analyzes key components with expectations of upcoming releases. **$**

The Forex Report analyzes foreign exchange market activity with a focus on key currencies and an overview of trading volume and activity. **$**

7.4.5.5
Ask Mr. Fed Forum   **ASKFED**

The Ask Mr. Fed Forum enables you to ask relevant questions of economists who are in touch with the inner workings of government activities. **$**

7.5
Micro Software Interfaces   **INTERFACES**

This section describes software interfaces that can increase the abilities of your personal computer to interact with CompuServe.

7.5.1
Specialized Software Interfaces   **MMM-56**

Specialized Software Interfaces contains two customized programs for computer-to-computer transfer of financial data. MQINT (GO MQINT) retrieves pricing information, and IQINT (GO IQINT) retrieves company account items.

7.5.1.4
MQINT   MQINT

MQINT is designed to meet the needs of microcomputer software that automates the downloading process. CompuServe guarantees an unchanging dialog within the program, with all prompts ending in a colon. MQINT allows access to the MicroQuote II, Quick Quote, and Commodity databases. Subscribers may select to retrieve single-day quotes for one or several issues or a time-series of quotes for a single issue or contract. The program minimizes data transmission time and employs a check sum if requested to assure correct data. See Appendixes D, E, F, G and H for lists of symbols used in this product.

     Updated daily. **$**

7.5.1.5
IQINT   IQINT

IQINT, like MQINT, is designed for program-controlled downloading to your microcomputer. IQINT, however, retrieves descriptive items about the specified issue from MicroQuote II, company financial information from Disclosure II and earnings information from I/B/E/S. See Appendix F for a list of optionable stocks.

     Updated daily. **$**

7.5.3
The World of Lotus   LOTUS

The World of Lotus is sponsored and maintained by the Lotus Development Corporation to provide support to users of Lotus products and information about Lotus products and services. It includes news releases and other company information from Lotus, a list of software books and periodicals that complement Lotus products, technical product information, and answers to commonly asked questions. It provides "electronic distribution" of new device drivers, problem fixes and other technical information. Also included in the World of Lotus are the 1-2-3 Users Forum, the Symphony Users Forum, and the Jazz Users Forum all of which feature communication with Lotus product support as well as with other Lotus users.

7.5.3.6
Lotus 1-2-3 User Forum   LOTUS123

Lotus Development Corporation established the 1-2-3 Users Forum as part of the World of Lotus, and it is maintained by Lotus staff members. The forum provides registered members with the ability to:

- Read and leave messages to other members and to Lotus Development Corporation
- Upload and download applications software from the public domain libraries
- Share interests with other 1-2-3 members and
- Participate in online conferences.

7.5.3.7
Lotus Symphony User Forum   **SYMPHONY**

The Symphony Users Forum is similar to the 1-2-3 Users Forum except that the subject matter is geared to Lotus Symphony.

7.5.3.8
Lotus Graphics Products Forum   **LOTUSGRAPHIC**

Users of Freelance, Freelance Plus, and Graphwriter can exchange ideas in the Lotus Graphics Products Forum. Members discuss graphic business communication such as charts, diagrams, word charts, freehand drawings, symbols, and maps. Data libraries contain public domain software and symbols. A catalog of member interests and specialties can put you in touch with compatible fellow members.

7.5.3.9
Lotus Jazz Users Forum   **LOTUSJAZZ**

The Jazz Development Forum is the third forum in the World of Lotus. Like the 1-2-3 Users Forum and the Symphony Users Forum, registered members can:

- Read and leave messages to other members and to the Lotus Development Corporation
- Upload and download applications software from the public domain data library
- Share interest with other 1-2-3 members and
- Participate in online conferencing.

7.5.4
File Transfer   **MMM-17**

FILTRN, CompuServe's file transfer program, facilitates accurate transfer of data files from your microcomputer to CompuServe, and from CompuServe to your microcomputer. "B" protocol, which is supported by CompuServe's VIDTEX software, and XMODEM protocol are available to ensure accurate transfer. Additional information is available on VIDTEX (GO VIDTEX).

7.6
Personal Finance/Insurance   **FINANCE**

This section includes many services and programs that are useful for your personal financial and insurance decisions.

7

7

7.6.1
Social Security Administration   **SSA**
The Social Security Database provides information on the benefits programs available through Social Security including how to build up coverage, and eligibility for retirement, disability and Medicare benefits.

7.6.2
The Donoghue Moneyletter   **DON**
Nationally syndicated newspaper columnist and author William E. Donoghue offers financial advice for consumers. His newsletters include advice on banks, investment strategies, money market investments, mutual funds, loans, taxes, government regulations and retirement.

7.6.3
Independent Insurance   INS

The Insurance Consumer Information Service is produced by the Independent Insurance Agents of America and provides basic property and casualty insurance information. It tells you how to shop for insurance and how to file a claim. It has information on automobile, motorcycle, homeowners, renters and landlord insurance. There are sections on personal and professional liability. You can also order additional information to answer your insurance questions.

7.6.4
Shareholder Freebies   FRE

Shareholder Freebies informs current and prospective shareholders of the myriad of reductions and bargains available from the issuing company. Included are such items as reduced motel fees, trial packages of products, and welcome packs for shareholders attending meetings.

7.6.5
Rapaport's Diamond Service   RDC

Rapaport Diamond Corporation provides information about diamonds and the diamond trade and enables professionals to buy and sell diamonds. It gives background and general information about diamonds, detailed price information on diamond trading, a trading section that lists stones currently for sale as well as buy requests, diamond market reports, special diamond reports, letters to the system and auction reviews. Registered traders can update the database and have access to additional diamond data.

7.6.6
Calculating Personal Finances   FINTOL

This section offers products which enable you to balance your checkbook, calculate your net worth, and generate a loan amortization schedule.

7.6.6.1
Checkbook Balancer Program   CHECKBOOK

The checkbook balancing program enables you to balance your checkbook. After the initial run, the program is basically menu driven.

7.6.6.2
Calculate Your Net Worth   HOM-16

The Personal Net Worth Program uses on online questionnaire to create a detailed report of your assets, liabilities and total net worth.

7.6.6.3
Mortgage Calculator   **HOM-17**

The Loan Amortization Program will customize a detailed amortization schedule based on your loan criteria.

7.6.7
American Express® ADVANCE   **AXP**

American Express® Advance offers a series of online services including financial management programs for individual cardmembers and corporations. Examples of their services include account balance information and travel expense records. Travel services include information and reservations for tours and vacations around the world. Shopping services are also available.

7.6.8
Information USA/Finance   **IUS-1332**

Modern consumers need to know how to manage their money, and the U.S. government has many publications available on finance. You can learn about banking, consumer credit laws, safeguarding your investment and bill collection. Borrowing money is explained in publications on credit, types of loans, loan applications and interest rates.

7.6.9
U.S. Government Publications   **GPO**

There are two basic parts to this program. The first is a catalog of government publications, books, and subscription services. In addition to providing ordering information, any CompuServe Subscriber with a valid Master Charge or Visa card can order online any publication handled by the Government Printing Office. The orders are compiled and forwarded directly to the Government Printing Office at least once a week and more frequently as volume dictates.

The second part has online consumer information articles from government publications including articles on personal finance, health and fitness, automotive topics, food preparation and storage, parent and child, energy conservation and consumer notes. The entire database is updated weekly or as important changes occur.

7.7
Financial Forums   **FINFORUM**

This section contains financial forums. The Financial Forums enable you to ask specific questions about financial matters such as the economy, or about technical matters such as running Lotus Symphony. You'll be asking professionals who know their subject matter well, and you will have a chance to trade ideas with others like yourself.

7.7.1
Investors Forum   **INVFORUM**

The Investor's Forum is an area on CompuServe where anyone interested in the financial world may discuss topics of interest. The forum is administered by Forum Administrators who are well-versed in financial terms and strategies. A regularly scheduled real-time conference allows members to speak together about a myriad of financial topics. While many members are brokers or bankers, all are welcome.

7.7.2
NAIC Forum   **NAIC**

The goal of the National Association of Investors Forum is to educate long-term investors in how to find quality companies and buy stocks at good prices. Well-managed companies are identified from reported financial data and in-depth analysis. Members can share information on portfolio management, software, and favorite stocks.

7.7.3
Ask Mr. Fed Forum   **ASKFED**

The Ask Mr. Fed Forum enables you to ask relevant questions of economists who are in touch with the inner workings of government activities. **$**

7.7.4
Javelin Forum   **JAVELIN**

Javelin Software's business analysis and reporting system uses a more structured approach to model building than the traditional spreadsheet. The Javelin Forum helps you take full advantage of Javelin's capabilities. These capabilities include the ability to "look behind the numbers" to determine where a specific number comes from and view problems in several ways including worksheets, formulas, and presentation-quality graphs. Members of Javelin Software Corporation are online to answer your questions and provide technical support.

7.7.5
Lotus 1-2-3 User Forum   **LOTUS123**

Refer to 7.5.3.6

7.7.6
Lotus Graphics Forum   **LOTUSGRAPHIC**

Refer to 7.5.3.8

7.7.7
Lotus Jazz Users Forum   **LOTUSJAZZ**
Refer to 7.5.3.9

7.7.8
Lotus Symphony Users Forum   **SYMPHONY**
Refer to 7.5.3.7

7.7.9
Monogram Software Forum   **MONOGRAM**
Users of Monogram's software products, including Dollars and Sense and Moneyline, can use this forum to exchange information and applications. The data libraries are managed by Monogram Software's technical support and analysis department. The libraries contain answers to commonly asked questions, as well as examples of stock transactions, billing applications, credit card management and payroll administration. Monogram compatibility with IBM, Apple, Macintosh and Atari is also discussed.

7.8
MicroQuote II   **MQUOTE**

This menu choice accesses CompuServe's MicroQuote II database in command mode. If you are not familiar with this service, you may wish to use menu choice 1 (GO QUOTES) which accesses this information using menus.

MicroQuote II is designed for regular subscribers of CompuServe financial services who prefer the speed and efficiency of MicroQuote II where one can operate in "command mode", build files of issues, and run specific analyses in an expert mode. All of the information available under menu options or GO commands such as DISCLOSURE, QUOTES, RETURN, S&P, and TICKER is available in MicroQuote II, although the formats and the ways in which the reporting system works may be different.

You may wish to order the CompuServe Securities Information System Users Guide to learn more about the capabilities available in this area. Your order can be placed by typing GO ORDER.

MicroQuote II is updated continually on current quotes and daily on historical quotes. **$**

Stock Data Retrieval   **MQUOTE**

Stock Data Retrieval is available only by entering the command DATA when using Micro-Quote II command mode. It enables you to build files of historical security information for downloading to your microcomputer. Price and volume data is displayed showing the company, the date, and subscriber-specified choice of vollume, high/ask, low/bid, close/average, and sequence number. Dividend data and descriptive items are available as well as data on equity issues, debt issues, and options. Updated daily. **$**

7.9
Business News   **BUSNEWS**

This section contains business news services. It is a way for the busy executive to catch up on the latest business news.

7.9.1
AP Videotex   **APV**

The latest news from Associated Press updated hourly. It includes weather, national news, Washington news, world news, political happenings, entertainment, business news, Wall Street news, Dow Jones averages, features, sports and today in history.

7.9.2
Online Today Electronic Edition   OLT

The Electronic Edition of CompuServe's *Online Today* magazine. The *Online Today Electronic Edition* provides daily updated computer and information industry news, CompuServe news, product announcements, reviews of new hardware, software, books and more.

7.9.2.7
Online Today Online Inquiry   OLI

You can request general information about an ad displayed in *Online Today* and request product literature directly from advertisers.

7.9.4
The Business Wire   TBW

The Business Wire makes available press releases, news articles and other information from the world of business. It is updated continuously throughout the day and brings information on hundreds of different companies.

7.10
Instructions/Fees   FINHLP

This section contains information on electronic documentation, enables you to review your session charges and lists current transaction charges.

7.10.1
Electronic Documentation   IQD

You can access electronic documentation on CompuServe financial products.

7.10.2
Review Your Session Charges

You can itemize any surcharges incurred for financial products used during your current connect session.

7.10.4
Ticker and CUSIP Lookup   CUSIP
Refer to 7.1.7.1

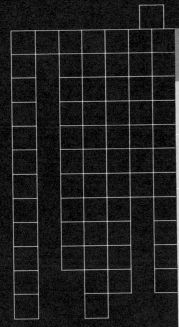

This chapter contains many different types of games. Some games are for one player against the computer. For others, like MegaWars I and III, you interact with other players, either as allies or enemies. This ability to interact and communicate with other players while you are playing the games is unique to CompuServe. We think that you will find our new-technology games exciting and challenging as well as a lot of fun.

Most games do not require special equipment. However, some are enhanced if the subscriber has VIDTEX or a recognized terminal emulator which supports cursor control.

8.1
Introduction to CompuServe Games   GAM-222
Newcomers can use the Introduction as a guide to the world of CompuServe Games. It explains game requirements, lists quick reference words for games and explains how to use the help facility.

8.1.4
Gaming Connection   GAMECON
The Gaming Connection is your gateway to three forums: ELECTRONIC GAMER (GO EGAMER), the Gamers' Forum (GO GAMERS) and Multi-Player Games Forum (GO MPGAMES).

8.1.4.1
ELECTRONIC GAMER™   EGAMER
The ELECTRONIC GAMER™ is an online magazine for all people who are interested in games. Updated twice monthly, TEG is staffed by editors who are expert gamers. Included in TEG are complete step-by-step "walkthrus" of popular computer games (such as the ZORK series by Infocom and the ULTIMA series by Lord British). A game hints section is available for players who want a nudge in the right direction rather than an explicit answer. New game reviews are continuously added to the magazine. "TFG's Gazette" is a magazine within a magazine and contains articles previously published in print magazines, commentary, humor, and fiction. If you're interested in games, The ELECTRONIC GAMER™ will inform and entertain you.

8

8.1.4.2
The Gamers' Forum   **GAMERS**

It's a computer game player's dream: an electronic forum dedicated to the communication, support and entertainment needs of the CompuServe game-playing community.

Activity conducted in this forum encompasses games conducted outside the CompuServe environment, games conducted via the Gamers' Forum conference area and message boards, and single-player games conducted within the CompuServe environment. If you have any questions or would like to discuss such games with other persons via a public forum, this is the place to do it.

8.1.4.3
The Multi-Players Games Forum   **MPGAMES**

An online forum dedicated to the communication, support, and entertainment needs of people who play any of the multi-player games via CompuServe's online environment. As a result of their multi-player nature and the complexity of the games' content, the games are rather challenging.

Players who have questions about any of the multi-player games are encouraged to use the forum to get answers to those questions from other players and from the Games' Forum Administrators. The forum serves as an exchange of ideas and hints to help you play the games. It also provides players with a way to communicate with teammates to plan strategy and to conduct online conference meetings.

8.2
Adventure Games   **ADVENT**

CompuServe has an outstanding collection of games for the adventurous game player.

8.2.1
British Legends   LEGENDS

As an adventurer in the multiplayer game British Legends, you will explore a land filled with mystery . . . dense forests, an island, a cottage and much more . . . in addition to the computer-generated and human characters you will encounter. Like all the multiplayer games, your play is influenced and enhanced by the presence of other players, but unlike other multiplayer games, well, take heed of these words of wisdom: "Life is never quite what it seems in 'British Legends'."

The goal of the game is to collect treasures, score points, and reach the enviable, honorable status of "Wizard." Once you reach this level of expertise, you are endowed with wondrous magical powers: the ability to become invisible, commit mischievous acts and more.

In other words, British Legends is not an ordinary adventure game. It embodies a vast, fantastic world of its own.

8.2.2
CastleQuest   CQUEST

Picture yourself on a long-awaited vacation to Romania's legendary Carpathian Mountains. During your trip your car breaks down, and you can't find help. You walk a long time and make it to a castle perched on the summit of a rocky rise above the road. You pound on the thick wooden door. Nobody answers, but the door slowly swings open. As you enter the castle you realize that you are very sleepy. You stumble up the stairs and collapse on a bed. When you awaken, your adventure begins.

The goal of this game is to thoroughly explore the castle, kill the master, loot the castle of its treasures, and accumulate points as the game progresses. To win, you must survive the many dangers you will encounter and reach the castle storeroom to store your treasures. Reaching the storeroom is not an easy task. In fact, it can be deadly.

Good Luck!

8

8.2.3
The House of Banshi   BANSHI

It's a game that takes you on a treasure-seeking journey through a dungeon. You begin outside of a large white house that is the center of your explorations. There is a mailbox in front of you. Open it and read what's inside before you begin exploring. As you explore, try to remember any unusual features of the terrain. They are handy later in your quest. To get full credit for the treasure you find, remove the treasures from the dungeon and deposit them safely in the trophy case in the living room of the House of Banshi. As you travel seeking the treasures, you'll encounter all sorts of villains and objects that interfere with your goal.

The House of Banshi is a game in which a working knowledge of myths and fables is helpful in solving the many puzzles within the mansion and its neighborhood. If you're familiar with computer adventure games, you'll recognize the plot of this game; the House of Banshi is CompuServe's version of the popular original game of Zork.

8.2.4
Original Adventure   **ORADVENT**

Adventure is actually two games — Original Adventure and New Adventure. The new game is a "larger" version of the Original Adventure which sparked all other versions, both micro and mainframe.

Both games are tests of your imagination, tests of your courage. The scene is a forest in which lies Colossal Cave. Most of your adventuring takes place within the cave, though there are also treasures above ground in New Adventure.

You begin your adventure outside a small well house. This is the center of your activities, and it is where you store your treasures. The entrance to the cave is south of the building, but you'll want to investigate the interior of the house before you leave for the cave.

The object of both games is to overcome the cave's deadly challenges as you explore it, collect its numerous treasures, and deposit them in the well house. It sound simple, but danger lurks with every turn. And remember: the cave in New Adventure contains more treasures than the one in Original Adventure. Thus you can score up to 751 points as opposed to 350 in Original Adventure.

8.2.5
New Adventure   **NEWADVENT**

8.2.6
Scott Adams' New Adventures   **ADAMS**

The Scott Adams Adventure Series offers an ideal way to introduce yourself to online computer adventure games. The games in the series vary in difficulty, and generally, the higher the number of the game, the more difficult it is. You may venture through Claymorgue Castle or control super heroes, but wherever you go or whatever game you play, you are searching for valuable treasures, or trying to perform a specific task. If you grow weary of searching, you can "save" your place in the game and return to it later. But you'll probably want to keep on playing until you've tried all of the games in the series.

8.3
Board/Parlor Games   **BPGAMES**

If you have a few minutes, come into our parlor and look over our collection of parlor and board games. Most are short and can be enjoyed with little instruction. Its a fun area for the entire family.

8.3.1
Astrology Calculator   **ASTROLOGY**

The Astrology Calculator is a tool for astrologers and would-be astrologers. Given the date, time, and place of birth, it performs all of the calculations necessary to generate a star chart. Try it. You may discover things about yourself that you never knew, or things that might otherwise remain a mystery forever.

8.3.2
Baffle   **BAFFLE**

Baffle enables you to test your vocabulary, learn new words, or both. The object is to form words using adjacent letters that appear on a 4 x 4 display. The trick is to find as many words as possible in three minutes. It's not as simple as you may think. As a matter of fact, it's downright BAFFLING.

8.3.3
Biorhythms   **BIORHYTHM**

Biorhythms helps you figure out what your emotional, mental, and physical state is and will be. It plots personalized charts for any month or series of months within a given year, and it provides a written analysis of each month. Biorhythms also features NAPLPS graphics and Run-Length Encoded (RLE) graphics capabilities.

8.3.4
Casino Blackjack   **MPBLACK**

Pit your luck and skill against other players as you try to get a card hand that adds up as closely as possible to 21 without going over. It's an ideal game if you are an avid gambler because you can flex your muscles and practice on your gambling savvy without losing any actual money. On the other hand, you can't win any either! What you DO win is an opportunity to meet, play with, send messages to, and receive messages from other CompuServe subscribers. If you are a novice gambler, it will improve your gambling know-how and prepare you for future trips to the gambling meccas of Las Vegas and Atlantic City.

8

8.3.5
Hangman   **HANGMAN**

The computerized version of the famous game that both children and adults enjoy. You play against the computer which selects the word, and you make the guesses until the poor man is hung or until you guess the correct word. Playing this game helps you find out how large your vocabulary is. It might also teach you a new word or two. If you are very good you may reach the Hall of Fame.

Hangman may be played on any terminal, but the display is much enhanced if you are using VIDTEX or other communications software with cursor control capabilities.

8.3.6
Interactive Chess   CHESS

The ancient game of kings can now be played the modern way — interactively with other chess players from around the world. Interactive Chess consists of a parlor, a spectator gallery area, and several game tables. You can enter the parlor, watch others play, and when you are ready, you can play on the board displayed on your terminal. Yet whether you choose to watch or play, you may communicate with the opponents and gallery members during the game.

8.4
Fantasy Role-Playing Games   FRPGAMES

If you are in the mood for a fantasy adventure where you assume the identity of another person or character, try out one or more of the fantasy role-playing games.

8.4.1
BlackDragon   BLACKDRAGON

Enter a magical, multilevel Labyrinth filled with treasure, but beware of the deadly creatures, traps, and pits that infest it. This fantasy role-playing game lets you accumulate treasures which, when converted to "experience points", add to the strength you'll need to make it through the maze alive and to conquer the evil Arch Demon. If you can make it through all levels of the maze, you are admitted to the Explorer's Hall of Fame for all to admire.

8.4.2
Castle Telengard   CASTLE

Adventure, treasure, and fearsome creatures await you in the Castle Telengard as you explore its 20 floors, accumulating wealth, building your experience, and searching for the mysterious Orb of Power. You can fight and cast spells to achieve your goals, and you'll need a combination of savvy, daring, intelligence, and plain ol' luck to conquer the challenges you'll encounter.

If you take this trip through the castle, take a map, or more accurately, make a map. Castle Telengard contains 8,000 locations, and you'll need a map to find your way out of this huge conglomeration of mortar and stone.

8.4.4
Island of Kesmai   ISLAND

Many years ago, a group of magicians wanted to escape persecution. They settled on the Island of Kesmai where they experimented in the black arts. They created many strange creatures through their sorcery, which took place in catacombs deep underground. As their anger and their pride grew over the years, they determined to have revenge on their persecutors by calling up an ancient Dragon of Droon. They produced the dragon, but they were not able to control it.

The dragon destroyed the laboratories and killed most of the magicians. It found its way to the temple located in the lowest levels of the catacombs, and it remains there to this day. Many of the creatures created in the laboratories escaped and have been living and multiplying ever since.

The Island of Kesmai is a multi-player fantasy role-playing game in which you direct your character around the Island and through its catacombs, searching for riches as you meet other players and trying to avoid the dangers of the island. On the Island of Kesmai, the dangers are many, the survivors are few, but the excitement is abundant.

8.5
Multi-Player Games   MULTIGAMES

This section contains games that can be played by more than one person. Since these games are played on CompuServe's network, you can be playing with or against other players from all over the country or even other parts of the world.

8.5.1
Air Traffic Controller   ATCONTROL

If you have nerves of steel and like the challenge of thinking at several levels at once, Air Traffic Controller could be your game. As an ATC, you're responsible for all planes within your sector of airspace. The object is to keep them from running out of fuel or crashing.

You must clear planes for arrival and landing while keeping track of those arriving from other sectors. Neighboring sectors may be controlled by other ATC players, challenging your communication skills as well as your nerves. Once you've built up your confidence, you can start again at an increased level of difficulty.

8.5.2
Baffle   **BAFFLE**
Refer to 8.3.2

8.5.3
Casino Blackjack   **MPBLACK**
Refer to 8.3.4

8.5.5
Island of Kesmai   **ISLAND**
Refer to 8.4.4

8.5.6
MegaWars I The Galactic Conflict   **MEGA1**
Imagine yourself at the helm of a starship, trying to capture planets and build an empire before the enemy destroys you and your effort. At your command are weapons such as phasers and photon torpedos and a bank of equipment on board to help you use them. The ship's radio lets you communicate with other members of you team or taunt the enemy into making a fatal mistake. In addition, as your skill increases you will rise in rank from cadet to admiral and gain the use of specialized ships.

8.5.7
MegaWars III The New Empire   **MEGA3**
Imagine yourself in a galaxy filled with strife and destruction. You find that you must have wealth and power in order to survive. But you can't get it by yourself. You need to join a team of people whose interests are similar to yours, people who want to expend their wealth and protect and manage what they have. So your team forms, but you are cautious because your team members may turn on you.

MegaWars III is a multi-player game which consists of two separate phases. The interactive phase is where you fly your ship about the Galaxy exploring for new planets to colonize and fighting with enemies. The second phase is an economic model, where you manipulate the economies and populations of the bases you own.

The game's starting point is its main menu. Here you may choose to build, repair, or fly your ship, manage your planets, and obtain game-related information. Throughout the game you may converse with other players who are playing at the same time. In addition, although many players form teams when they play the game, players can play it alone.

With these things in mind, you are ready to enter MegaWars III — The New Empire.

8.5.8
SeaWAR   SEAWAR

Adventure on the high seas. You're the commander of an armada of ships and you try to protect them on an enemy-infested ocean, scoring points as you destroy enemy battle-ships, submarines, aircraft carriers, and cruisers.

You can play singly against the computer, or against up to three human opponents. The object is to destroy all of your enemy's ships by commanding your own armada more skillfully.

The game of SeaWAR is divided into two parts: the War Room, where you meet and challenge opponents, and the game itself. In the War Room, players can talk to each other.

This multi-player war game combines the elements of war-room strategy and battle-ship strength, making it simple enough for novice game players and challenging enough for experienced game players.

8.5.9
SpaceWAR   SPACEWAR

SpaceWAR is a super fast-action multi-player shoot-'em-up war game in which only the quickest, most accurate fighting ships survive! It's a bit easier than the MegaWars games, but it's fast-action nature keeps you at the edge of your seat. You're pitted against all other players, and points are awarded for each ship that you hit. You can lose points for firing and missing, ramming another player, running into a star, and attempting to dock at an enemy base, so be careful! If you score enough points, you may be admitted to The Annals, a sort of "Hall of Fame" for high scorers.

8.5.10
You Guessed It!   YGI

You Guessed It! is a real-time, multi-player game show simulation, in which players form teams and answer general information and trivia questions. There's interaction between players, as well as with a cast of "online personalities." There is a lobby for meeting other players, a BIO feature, which lets you learn more about those playing, and a post-game lounge. Will you meet new friends, have fun, and discover the True Meaning of Life? You Guessed It!

8.6
Simulation/Sports Games   SSGAMES

Simulated games of football, golf and air traffic controller provide excitement for competi-tive players to test their skills from the comfort of their own terminals.

8

8.6.1
Advanced Digital Football   **ADFL**

Armchair athletes, push aside that popcorn. The Digital Football League has drafted you to coach your team in a simulated contest. You can select your team, your opponent, and level of coaching involvement. You can call offensive and defensive plays using established strategies, or be creative and invent your own.

8.6.2
Air Traffic Controller   **ATCONTROL**

Refer to 8.5.1

8.6.3
Football   **FOOTBALL**

It's fourth down and goal-to-go on the three-yard line. You're the coach for the offense. What play will you call? This is a situation you might encounter when playing CompuServe's version of Football. It can be played by one person or by two people at the same computer; you always play offense, while the computer plays defense. No matter who you're playing, you can never quite predict what they'll do.

8.6.4
Golf   GOLF
The average golfer must travel to a golf course to play. You, however, can play at your terminal on a championship 18-hole simulated layout. Your talent will lie in your intelligence, knowledge of the game, and your ability to keep your eye on the computerized ball.

8.7
Trivia/Thought Games   TTGAMES
These games will stretch your mind and test your knowledge.

8.7.1
Baffle   BAFFLE
Refer to 8.3.2

8.7.2
The Multiple Choice   MULTIPLECHOI
The Multiple Choice is a collection of tests that are designed to be fun. There really is something for everyone from kids to adults. It includes IQ tests, personality tests, trivia questions, a test that simulates the Miller Analogies test, sports tests, and even a touch-type tutor which provides 20 lessons for learning touch-typing on your computer at your own pace.

8.7.2.1.4
Slogans for Sale   SLOGANS
This trivia game in The Multiple Choice tests your knowledge of TV advertisements. Can you fill in the missing words when given part of the slogan? A high score can put your name on the honor roll of Madison Avenue Masters.

8

8.7.2.1.9
Stage II — Two Stage Trivia   STAGEII
Refer to 8.7.5

8.7.3
Science Trivia   SCITRIVIA

Is there a budding Einstein in the audience? Even if you missed the Nobel Prize this year, you can challenge the top scorers in the Science Trivia Hall of Fame. Test your knowledge of biology, chemistry, physics, and mathematics through the Science Trivia Quiz. The multiple choice questions are changed weekly. Questions and comments can be discussed in the Science/Math Forum (GO SCIENCE).

8.7.4
SHOWBIZQUIZ   SHOWBIZ

SHOWBIZQUIZ is a trivia game that tests your knowledge of the entertainment world in a variety of categories such as Frank Sinatra, the Twilight Zone or the Rolling Stones.

8.7.5
Stage II — Two Stage Trivia   STAGEII

Stage II is a trivia game whereby you answer three trivia questions and then look for a common theme in the answers. It can be played individually or as a group.

8.7.7
The Whiz Quiz   WHIZ

Do you think you are a knowledgeable person? The Whiz Quiz sponsored by Grolier's Academic American Encyclopedia will test your knowledge in a variety of categories including geography, current events, movies, sports, music, science, literature, history and myths and legends. Up to four people can play. The top ten scores for a session will enter the Wizard Hall of Fame.

8.7.8
Word Scramble   SCRAMBLE

Fi oyu acn keam nesse fo sethe dorws, ouy ilwl jneyo isth maeg.

The above sentence gives you a brief idea of how word scramble works: the computer scrambles the word and you get to unscramble it. If you score well, you may be eligible for the Hall of Fame.

You can play Word Scramble on any terminal, but the display is greatly enhanced if your communications software has cursor control capabilities.

Dogo cukl!

8.7.9
You Guessed It!   YGI
Refer to 8.5.10

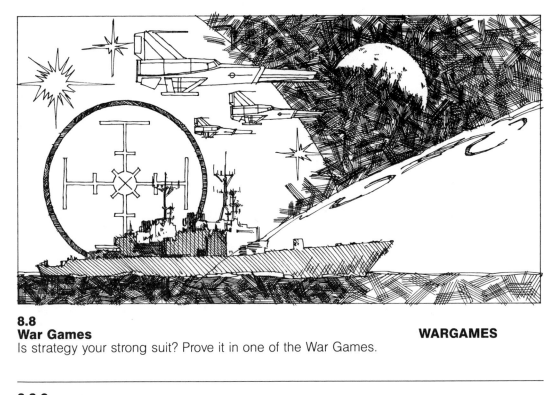

8.8
War Games   **WARGAMES**
Is strategy your strong suit? Prove it in one of the War Games.

8.8.2
MegaWars I The Galactic Conflict   **MEGA1**
Refer to 8.5.6

8.8.3
MegaWars III The New Empire   **MEGA3**
Refer to 8.5.7

8.8.4
SeaWAR   **SEAWAR**
Refer to 8.5.8

8.8.5
SpaceWAR   **SPACEWAR**
Refer to 8.5.9

8.9
Entertainment News/Information   **EGNEWS**
This section gives you the news on what's hot and what's not, in the world of entertainment.

8.9.1
Gaming Connection   **GAMECON**
Refer to 8.1.4

8.9.1.1
ELECTRONIC GAMER™   **EGAMER**
Refer to 8.1.4.1

8.9.1.2
The Gamers' Forum   **GAMERS**
Refer to 8.1.4.2

8.9.1.3
The Multi-Players Games Forum   **MPGAMES**
Refer to 8.1.4.3

8.9.2
Hollywood Hotline   **HOLLYWOOD**
Hollywood Hotline is a news and information service of noteworthy events in motion pictures, television programs and music recordings. It also includes a trivia quiz, entertainment features, photos of stars (GO HHA), and an entertainment encyclopedia which includes such things as past Academy and Tony award winners. Also included in this product are the movie reviewettes (GO MOVIES) and the SHOWBIZQUIZ (GO SHOWBIZ). To receive the photos you must be using VIDTEX or similar software with a computer with high resolution graphic capabilities. Updated daily. **$**

8.9.3
Movie Reviewettes   **MOVIES**
A thorough and witty treatment of the most recent movie releases. The movie rating guide makes finding a good movie easier.

8.9.5
RockNet   ROCK

RockNet provides the music enthusiast with up-to-the-minute news and information on the world of rock. It contains:

- The RockNet Forum (GO ROCKNET),
- Rock news,
- A list of top record reviews and
- Articles about rock music.

8.9.5.5
RockNet (Rock Music) Forum   ROCKNET

The RockNet Forum has many members that are within the record industry, and you may learn news items before they appear in newspapers.

8.9.6
Soap Opera Summaries   SOAPS

What did Erica do to Phoebe? What did Felicia say to the DA? And who was in bed with Clint? If you care about any of these questions, you should check out the Soap Opera Summaries. In addition to daily summaries, you will learn what is happening in real life to your favorite stars, cast lists, where to write to soap stars and fan club news. **$**

8.10
Entertainment/Games Forums   EGFORUMS

This section contains the forums for people who like to have fun by playing computer games.

8

8.10.1
CBIG (CB Interest Group)   CBIG

CBIG is the Special Interest Group for CBers. CBIG consists of a bulletin board and member and data libraries. There are sections for CB personal ads, technology, handles, etc., as well as several valuable programs for split screen CBing and viewing CBers' digitized pictures.

8.10.2
Comic Book Forum   COMIC

This forum features news, reviews and conferences with some of the greats of comic books and animations.

8.10.3
Consumer Electronics Forum   **CEFORUM**
The Consumer Electronics Forum is dedicated to exchanging information about electronic consumer products such as VCRs, telephone answering machines, compact disk players, and even earth station equipment. The forum features articles, reviews, new products and news in its data libraries. You can get answers for your questions and discuss the latest issues facing this industry. Special interactive online conferences feature guests from manufacturers such as Sony, Pioneer and Panasonic.

8.10.4
Gaming Connection   **GAMECON**
Refer to 8.1.4

8.10.4.1
The ELECTRONIC GAMER ™   **EGAMER**
Refer to 8.1.4.1

8.10.4.2
The Gamers' Forum   **GAMERS**
Refer to 8.1.4.2

8.10.4.3
Multi-Player Games Forum   **MPGAMES**
Refer to 8.1.4.3

8.10.5
General Music Forum   **MUSICFORUM**
The Music Forum is a forum for discussing classical, jazz, popular, blues, country and western, rock and foreign music. There are weekly conferences. The database contains live interviews done in the Music Forum, a top-40 countdown, computer music programs and articles about music.

8.10.6
Picture Support Forum   **PICS**
The Picture Support Forum is dedicated to expanding the availability of online graphics. This forum is for exchange of information on how to create and upload graphics files, to provide graphics files for those without the ability to create them, and to maintain a display area of graphics files for downloading. Members can share information about their techniques, tips and traps.

8.10.7
RockNet   **ROCK**
Refer to 8.9.5

8.10.7.5
RockNet Forum   **ROCKNET**
Refer to 8.9.5.5

8

8.10.8
Sci-Fi/Fantasy   **SCI**
Sci-Fi and Fantasy's forum serves the needs of people who are interested in science fiction and fantasy. You will find:

- The Science Fiction and Fantasy Forum (GO SCI-FI),
- The Comic Book Forum (GO COMIC),
- News about publishing, movie making, TV, conventions and
- Book reviews and commentaries.

8.10.8.1
Sci-Fi/Fantasy Forum   **SCI-FI**

The Sci-Fi Forum is a place where people who enjoy Science Fiction can get together and chat about their mutual likes and dislikes. There are also conferences with famous authors, producers and publishers.

8.10.8.2
Comic Book Forum   **COMIC**

Refer to 8.10.2

8.10.9
WitSIG   **WITSIG**

WitSIG is dedicated to humor and entertainment. It is a place where you can come to relax and have a laugh or two after visiting the more serious areas of CompuServe.

8.11
Order Games Manual   **ORDER**

Access CompuServe's online ordering service and place your order selecting from CompuServe's many exciting products — from users guides, T-shirts, game maps, posters and more. You can also check on an existing order's status and change an order before it is filled. You are not charged for connect time viewing descriptions or placing an order. You are, however, charged for communications surcharges.

8

Home Health Family	9
Food/Wine	9.1
Personal Finance	9.2
Health/ Fitness	9.3
The Electronic Mall/Shopping	9.4
Special Interest Forums	9.5
Hobbies	9.6
Art/Music/ Literature	9.7
Reference Material	9.8

This chapter contains information on food, wines, personal finances, hobbies, fitness and health. In addition, you can find reference and educational material and an Electronic Mall for your shopping convenience.

9.1
Food/Wine Forums   **FOOD**
This section contains forums for people who enjoy good food and wine.

9.1.1
Cook's Online   **COOKS**
This is a place where people can share their enthusiasm for cooking and gourmet food. Members swap recipes, exchange cooking tips and share menu planning ideas. Fine restaurants are discussed and members can consult with cooking experts online.

9.1.2
Bacchus Wine Forum   **WINEFORUM**
The Bacchus Wine Forum presents information on many wine-related topics. Information about your favorite wines may also be shared with other winelovers. Issues of *The Informed Enophile*, a wine newsletter, are included, and online wine-tasting parties are held regularly.

9.2
Personal Finance   **FINTOL**

This section offers products which enable you to balance your checkbook, calculate your net worth, and generate a loan amortization schedule.

9.2.1
Checkbook Balancer Program   **CHECKBOOK**

The checkbook balancing program enables you to balance your checkbook. After the initial run, the program is basically menu driven.

9.2.2
Calculate Your Net Worth   **HOM-16**

The Personal Net Worth Program uses on online questionnaire to create a detailed report of your assets, liabilities and total net worth.

9.2.3
Mortgage Calculator   **HOM-17**

The Loan Amortization Program will customize a detailed amortization schedule based on your loan criteria.

9.3
Health/Fitness   **HEALTH**

This section contains information on health-related matters including sports medicine, sexuality, mental health and general health topics.

9.3.1
HealthNet   **HNT**

HealthNet is a comprehensive online medical reference source. It contains a reference library, a bimonthly newsletter, and a subscriber inquiry forum. Also included is a section on sports medicine with information on nutrition, exercise and the benefits of and injuries incurred from some specific sports.

    HealthNet is updated continuously by a team of licensed, board-certified physicians.

9.3.2
Human Sexuality Forum   **HUMAN**

Human sexuality questions and problems are answered in an informative manner. Special features include articles on social skills, dating, relationships and sexual problems. Experts answer questions on a variety of topics. Two forums are available for subscribers to share their feelings, experiences and relationships with others in a warm, supportive environment.

9

9.3.2.5.1
HSX Support Group A   **HSX-100**

This forum is geared toward specific groups such as couples, parents, singles, women and gays.

9.3.2.5.2
HSX Support Group B   **HSX-200**

This forum focuses on specific topics such as passages, breaking up, encounter groups and bisexuality.

9.3.3
Good Earth Forum   GOODEARTH

The Good Earth Forum provides a place for subscribers to discuss topics which relate to natural living. Topics include gardening, horticulture, natural nutrition, and folkways. In addition, the forum provides a section for those who speak and write Esperanto.

9.3.4 Healthcom/Health Forum   HCM

Healthcom/Health Forum allows a subscriber to discuss health-related matters with other subscribers including topics on mental health, child care and sexuality. Subscribers also have access to biomedical literature through MEDLINE as well as current and accurate information on rare disorders and diseases through the NORD Services/Rare Disease Database. In addition, an AIDS quiz and AIDS reference library are available.

9.3.5
NORD Services/Rare Disease Database   NORD

The NORD Services/Rare Disease Database provides the subscriber with current and accurate information on rare disorders and diseases. Some topics covered include AIDS research, education for handicapped children, and information on digestive disease research centers. Subscribers also have access to biomedical literature through MEDLINE, and can communicate with other subscribers on various subjects. In addition, a NORD newsletter is available which explains NORD and presents news on the latest rare disease updates and facts.

9.3.6
PaperChase (MEDLINE)   PCH

PaperChase gives access to MEDLINE, the National Library of Medicine's database of references to biomedical literature. Included are over 5 million references from 3,400 journals which date from January 1966 through the current date. $*

9.3.7
Information USA/HEALTH   INFOUSA

Information USA tells you how to use the free or nearly free government publications and services that are available. It explains the art of obtaining information from bureaucrats and gives other helpful information when dealing with the government. Information USA was extracted from the reference book of the same name written by Matthew Lesko.

9.4
The Electronic MALL/Shopping   SHOPPING

This section contains the CompuServe products that enable you to shop in the comfort of your own home.

9.4.1
The Electronic Mall   **EM**
Please refer to Chapter 6 for information on the Electronic Mall.

9.4.2
Comp-u-store Online   **CUS**
Now you can join the thousands of other educated consumers who access America's largest discount electronic shopping service. Shop at home for more than 250,000 name-brand products — with savings of up to 50 percent.

Now you can access Comp-u-store OnLine as a CompuServe subscriber and browse through the electronic database for everything from air conditioners to computers to microwaves. Comp-u-store OnLine is your link to major manufacturers, wholesalers, and suppliers. That means that as a member you pay much less since costly retail price mark-ups, inventories and storefronts are eliminated. When you decide to buy, your low price includes delivery right to your door. There are no hidden costs. Your purchase comes in a factory-sealed carton with all manufacturer's warranties and guarantees in full effect.

The Comp-u-sttore OnLine shopping service does not end with the 250,000 product selection. While OnLine, visit Comp-u-mall — a collection of fine specialty shops offering something for everyone. Select fine foods from our Gourmet Food Shops, including Omaha Steaks, Hickory Farms and Double Truffle Chocolates. Looking for a special gift? Long Distant Roses, The E.A. Carey Smokeshop, Stanley Tools and 800 Spirits are just a few of the national retailers located in Comp-u-mall.

Comp-u-store OnLine's Auctions and Amusements offer you ways to have fun while saving money. Use your computer skills to solve our Scavenger Hunt and win valuable prizes. Participate in the weekly auctions to bid against other members across the U.S. and save hundreds of dollars on such items as TV's, VCR's, stereo equipment, sports equipment and more.

Comp-u-store OnLine's Consumer and Customer Service Areas were created with you in mind. Consumer Services include Classified Ads, Software Reviews, The Consumer Hotline and ERA Real Estate. The Information Booth, our Customer Service Center, is where you can send questions or offer suggestions. Learn about membership bonuses such as the free VISA card and Comp-u-bucks.

Visit Comp-u-store OnLine today, and you'll have a world of savings at your fingertips. The CompuServe Users Guide shows you how.

9

9.4.3
CompuServe's SOFTEX^{SM} Software Catalog   **SOFTEX**

CompuServe's SOFTEX^{SM} is an electronic software catalog which enables you to purchase and receive commercial software through your personal computer without the inconvenience of driving to a computer store or waiting for mail delivery. SOFTEX's growing selection includes popular commercially-available software as well as hard-to-find software from smaller vendors. Selections include programming utilities, tutorials, spreadsheets, accounting packages and games for most personal computers.

Your machine requires terminal software that supports an error-checking file transfer protocol, such as XMODEM or CompuServe's "B" protocol. Purchases are billed to your CompuServe account.

9.4.4
Order from CompuServe   **ORDER**

Access CompuServe's online ordering service and place your order selecting from CompuServe's many exciting products — from users guides, T-shirts, game maps, posters and more. You can also check on an existing order's status and change an order before it is filled. You are not charged for connect time viewing descriptions or placing an order. You are, however, charged for communications surcharges.

9.4.5
New Car Showroom   **NEWCAR**

New Car Showroom is a comparison shopping guide for consumers making new vehicle purchases. You can examine and compare features and specifications of passenger cars, trucks, vans and special-purpose vehicles. Over 700 foreign and domestic cars and trucks are compared in prices, standard and optional features and technical specifications, such as fuel economy and roominess.

9.4.6
Online Today Online Inquiry   **OLI**

You can request general information about an ad displayed in *Online Today* and request product literature directly from advertisers.

9.5
Special Interest Forums   **HOM-50**

This section contains forums where people share their ideas on topics that enrich lives such as religion, music, politics and sexuality.

9.5.1
Aquaria/Fish Forum   **FISHNET**
Aquarium professionals and hobbyists alike can join the Aquaria & Tropical Fish Forum to talk "fish." Members of fish specialty groups can exchange information on products, diseases and news. Join a live conference and meet fellow fish fanciers across the country.

Regular conferences are scheduled with some of the nation's best known aquarists. Questions to the Forum Administrator (SysOp) will be answered within 24 hours, but if you can't wait, a voice line is available.

9.5.2
Religion Forum   **RELIGION**
The Religion Forum is designed for people who like to share discussions, opinions and information, as well as ask questions, on topics which relate to religion. Forum members may meet new "friends" while expanding their theological horizons.

9.5.3
Working From Home Forum   **WORK**
The Working From Home Forum unites those who work from their homes with others who are in similar circumstances. It allows a subscriber to exchange information, make contacts, share resources and solutions to problems and meet other subscribers, as well as keep up-to-date on the latest home/office management tips, resources, laws, tax benefits, and marketing approaches.

9.5.4
National Issues/People Forum   **ISSUESFORUM**

The National Issues/People Forum is a forum for the free exchange of ideas about current issues and names in the news. There are sections for discussion of peace, politics, individualism, high tech, handicapped, paranormal, men and women's issues, youth and social issues. A number of regularly-scheduled conferences are held, and the data libraries contain many interesting articles, message threads and conference transcripts.

9.5.5
Military Veterans Services   **VET**

The Military Vets Forum encourages discussion of current topics, and includes a personal adjustment section for Vets to inquire about problems, data library files on veterans benefits, the MIA/POW issue, Agent Orange, Atomic Vets, Veterans Organizations and member writings. The complete list of the names on the Vietnam Veterans Memorial and a direct connection to CDC on the Agent Orange Studies is included. A CompuServe Forum and Buddy Locator are available to veterans only.

9.5.6
RockNet   **ROCK**

RockNet provides the music enthusiast with up-to-the-minute news and information on the world of rock. It contains:

- The RockNet Forum (GO ROCKNET),
- Rock news,
- A list of top record reviews and
- Articles about rock music.

9.5.6.5
RockNet (Rock Music) Forum   **ROCKNET**

The RockNet Forum has many members that are within the record industry, and you may learn news items before they appear in newspapers.

9.5.7
Food/Wine Forums   **FOOD**
Refer to 9.1

9.5.7.1
Cook's Online   **COOKS**
Refer to 9.1.1

9

9.5.7.2
Bacchus Wine Forum   **WINEFORUM**
Refer to 9.1.2

9.5.8
HamNet (Ham Radio) Online   **HAM**
HamNet Online is dedicated to serving the needs of amateur radio and short-wave listening (SWL) enthusiasts. You will find:

- Information on getting started in ham radio and SWL,
- The latest news and information on ham radio and SWL events,
- Regular "electronic editions" of amateur radio and SWL newsletters and
- Information on new technical developments.

9.5.8.3
HamNet (Ham Radio) Forum   **HAMNET**
This is the conferencing facility of HamNet Online and is where you can converse with others who are interested in amateur radio and short wave listening.

9.5.9
Auto Racing Forum   **RACING**
Auto Racing Forum provides the subscriber with driver biographies, track information, sanctioning organization addresses and contact information, schedules, and other information of interest to motorsports fans. In addition, real-time auto racing reports, filed directly from major events across the United States and Canada, are included.

9.5.10
ModelNet   **MODELNET**
The Model Aviation Forum is a forum for the model hobbyist. Builders of model railroads, airplanes, cars and boats will find all these disciplines covered in the forum. In addition, forum members have access to newsletters and articles from "Model Aviation Magazine" and a complete contest calendar. A "Swap Shop" enables hobbyists to trade parts.

9

9.5.11
Human Sexuality Forum   **HUMAN**
Refer to 9.3.2

9.5.11.5.1
HSX Support Group A   **HSX-100**
Refer to 9.3.2.5.1

9.5.11.5.2
HSX Support Group B   **HSX-200**
Refer to 9.3.2.5.2

9.5.12
Sci-Fi/Fantasy   **SCI**
Sci-Fi and Fantasy's forum serves the needs of people who are interested in science fiction and fantasy. You will find:

- The Science Fiction and Fantasy Forum (GO SCI-FI),
- The Comic Book Forum (GO COMIC),
- News about publishing, movie making, TV, conventions and
- Book reviews and commentaries.

9.5.12.1
Sci-Fi/Fantasy Forum   **SCI-FI**
The Sci-Fi Forum is a place where people who enjoy Science Fiction can get together and chat about their mutual likes and dislikes. There are also conferences with famous authors, producers and publishers.

9.5.13
General Music Forum   **MUSICFORUM**
The Music Forum is a forum for discussing classical, jazz, popular, blues, country and western, rock and foreign music. There are weekly conferences. The database contains live interviews done in the Music Forum, a top-40 countdown, computer music programs and articles about music.

9.5.14
Good Earth Forum   **GOODEARTH**
Refer to 9.3.3

9

9.5.15
Literary Forum   **LITFORUM**

The Literary Forum is a gathering place for professional writers, literature readers, journalists, humorists, and those with an interest in any related field. Included are sections on poetry, controversial topics, fiction discussions, science fiction, comics, humor and journalism.

9.5.16
Outdoor Forum   **OUTDOORFORUM**

The Great Outdoors provides outdoor lovers with an avenue to converse and share information with other outdoor lovers. Areas and topics of information include camping, climbing, backpacking, fishing, hunting, cycling, sailing, and winter sports. In addition, search and rescue, nature, wildlife, equipment reviews and park and campground information is included.

9.5.17
Consumer Electronics Forum   **CEFORUM**

The Consumer Electronics Forum is dedicated to exchanging information about electronic consumer products such as VCRs, telephone answering machines, compact disk players, and even earth station equipment. The forum features articles, reviews, new products and news in its data libraries. You can get answers for your questions and discuss the latest issues facing this industry. Special interactive online conferences feature guests from manufacturers such as Sony, Pioneer and Panasonic.

9.5.18
Healthcom/Health Forum   **HCM**

Refer to 9.3.4

9.6
Hobbies   **HOBBIES**

This section includes information on those activities people pursue for pleasure such as sailing, photography, ham radio, model building and tropical fish. In addition, an area is devoted to those who are interested in outdoor activities.

9

9.6.1
Photography Forum   **PHOTOFORUM**

Shutterbugs of all levels, professional and amateur, can meet in the Photography Forum. Members can discuss photography equipment, film types, and camera techniques. Professionals can communicate with others in the business and share money-making ideas.

9.6.2
Aquaria/Fish Forum
Refer to 9.5.1

FISHNET

9.6.3
Outdoor Forum
Refer to 9.5.16

OUTDOORFORUM

9.6.4
ModelNet
Refer to 9.5.10

MODELNET

9.6.5
HamNet (Ham Radio) Online
Refer to 9.5.8

HAM

9.6.5.3
HamNet (Ham Radio) Forum
Refer to 9.5.8.3

HAMNET

9.6.6
Sailing Forum

SAILING

Ahoy sailors! Sea dogs interested in staying downwind of current events should join the Sailing Forum. Members will share information and opinions about all aspects of sailing including equipment, racing, and favorite cruising spots.

9.6.7
Comic Book Forum

COMIC

This forum features news, reviews and conferences with some of the greats of comic books and animations.

9.6.8
Astronomy Forum   **ASTROFORUM**
Amateur or professional stargazers can join cosmic forces with fellow astronomers
from around the world. Beginners with a universe of questions can learn about hardware
or techniques. Professionals can take advantage of the Astronomy Forum to rapidly disseminate information among colleges. Members of all levels can learn about national or
international special events of interest. Archives contain public domain astronomy software
and quality reference articles.

9.7
Art/Music/Literature   **ARTS**
This section is dedicated to literature and science-fiction fans as well as to music lovers of
all kinds.

9.7.1
Literary Forum   **LITFORUM**
Refer to 9.5.15

9.7.2
Sci-Fi/Fantasy   **SCI**
Refer to 9.5.12

9.7.2.1
Sci-Fi/Fantasy Forum   **SCI-FI**
Refer to 9.5.12.1

9.7.3
General Music Forum   **MUSICFORUM**
Refer to 9.5.13

9.7.4
RockNet   **ROCK**
Refer to 9.5.6

9.7.4.5
RockNet (Rock Music) Forum   **ROCKNET**
Refer to 9.5.6.5

9.8
Reference Material   **REFERENCE**
Please refer to Chapter 10 for information on Reference Material and Education.

9

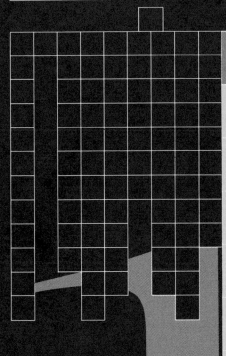

Reference Education	10
IQuest	10.1
Academic American Encyclopedia	10.2
Government Information	10.3
Demographics	10.4
Other Reference Sources	10.5
Services for Educators	10.6
Services for the Handicapped	10.7
Services for Students/Parents	10.8
Trivia/ Thought Games	10.9
Educational Forums	10.10

This section includes general information of interest such as an encyclopedia, a directory of public officials and U.S. government publications. In addition, educational material is presented devoted to services for educators, the handicapped, students and parents.

10.1
IQuest   IQU

IQuest, CompuServe's online information retrieval service, provides easy access to more than 800 databases from companies such as Dialogue, BRS, NewsNet, Vu/text, and ADP. All types of information are included. From scholarly to popular press, business-related to the obscure, IQuest is the most comprehensive source of online information anywhere.

IQuest contains fully indexed historical data and is updated electronically each day. Both bibliographic and full-text documents are available. Source materials include magazines, newspapers, indexes, conference proceedings, directories, books, newsletters, government documents, dissertations, encyclopedias, patent records, and reference guides.

All IQuest databases are accessible via the same easy-to-use, menu-driven format. No training is required. IQuest offers two simple ways to retrieve information:

- IQuest-I will choose the appropriate database once a subscriber has selected a topic and
- IQuest-II allows a subscriber to go directly to a specified database.

    Free, online, real-time help is available in IQuest by typing SOS. **$**

10.2
Academic Am. Encyclopedia   ENCYCLOPEDIA
The online edition of Grolier's Academic American Encyclopedia is filled with the latest in science, technology, politics, business, law, the arts, and social sciences as well as the whole range of historical data associated with a top-ranked encyclopedia. It is a 21 volume general reference source of over 30,000 articles and ten million words that is updated and revised four times a year. **$**

10.3
Government Information   GOVERNMENT
Government Information includes a directory of public officials as well as material on government publications.

10.3.1
Information USA   INFOUSA
Information USA tells you how to use the free or nearly free government publications and services that are available. It explains the art of obtaining information from bureaucrats and gives other helpful information when dealing with the government. Information USA was extracted from the reference book of the same name written by Matthew Lesko.

10.3.1.12
Electronic Answer Man   EAM
Do you want to study overseas? How do you patent your invention? Are pests destroying your organic garden? The Electronic Answer Man can help you on almost any topic. EAM describes government publications, public agency departments, and funding sources.

10.3.2
Government Publications   GPO
There are two basic parts to this program. The first is a catalog of government publications, books and subscription services. In addition to providing ordering information, any CompuServe Subscriber with a valid Master Charge or Visa card can order online any publication handled by the Government Printing Office. The orders are compiled and forwarded directly to the Government Printing Office at least once a week and more frequently as volume dictates.

    The second part has online consumer information articles from government publications including articles on personal finance, health and fitness, automotive topics, food preparation and storage, parent and child, energy conservation and consumer notes. The entire database is updated weekly or as important changes occur.

10

10.3.2.4
FBI Ten Most Wanted   **FBI**
The FBI's current Ten Most Wanted Fugitives are listed including biographical information, crimes and pictures. It also gives information on FBI past fugitives including stories of their apprehensions. To obtain the fugitives' pictures, your terminal must support the graphics mode.

10.4 Demographics   **DEMOGRAPHICS**
This section enables you to obtain demographic information for any area of the United States. Information includes the population as well as the income, age, and race of the residents. The data is based on the 1980 Census, and current year and five-year forecasts.

10.4.2
Neighborhood Report   **NEIGHBORHOOD**
The Neighborhood Report provides a summary of the demographic makeup of any Zip Code in the United States. Population, race, and age breakdowns are displayed on the report as well as the household income distribution, the types of households, and the occupations of the residents of the neighborhood. Housing patterns for the neighborhood are also examined with the status of occupied housing, average home value and rent, and the age of housing structures shown on the report.
    The Neighborhood Report carries a surcharge per Zip Code. With the Neighborhood Report prospective home buyers or apartment dwellers can research areas to which they are considering moving. Similarly, home sellers can determine the most favorable selling points of their current Zip Codes. An 80-column printer is needed for printing reports. Updated annually. **$**

10.4.4
US-State-County Reports   **USSTCN**
The US-State-County Demographic Profiles provides summaries of the demographic makeup of the entire United States, or any state or county. The profile gives population data, race and age breakdowns, household income distribution, types of households, and occupations of residents in the defined area. In addition, the status of occupied housing, average home value and rent, and the age of housing structures are reported. The US-State-County Profiles carry a surcharge per report. With these reports you can compare a Zip Code report, generated by the Neighborhood Report, to its county or state. An 80-column printer is needed for printing reports. Updated annually. **$**

10

10.4.5
SUPERSITE   **SUPERSITE**
SUPERSITE demographic information from CACI is available for the entire U.S., and every state, county, SMSA, Arbitron TV Market (ADI), Nielsen TV Market (DMA), Place, Census Tract, Minor Civil Division (MCD) and Zip Code in the United States. Demographic reports are provided covering general demographics, income, housing, education, employment and current and five-year forecasts. In addition, sales potential reports for major types of retail stores can be generated.

ACORN Target Marketing profiles and potentials are also available. ACORN, A Classification of Residential Neighborhoods, classifies all households in the U.S. into 44 market segments based on the demographic, socioeconomic, and housing characteristics of the neighborhoods. The ACORN Market Potential Reports are created by linking the ACORN clusters to syndicated national surveys.

Each report in SUPERSITE is surcharged, and you will be shown the cost of your requested reports before they are run to give you the opportunity to abort the run before incurring any surcharges. An 80-column printer is needed for printing reports. Updated annually. **$E**

10.5
Other Reference Sources   **EDU-6**
This section contains a collection of reference sources that can help you with homework, buy a car or even help locate missing children.

10.5.2
Missing Children   **MIS**
Missing Children is a service provided by the National Child Safety Council to assist in locating abducted children. The missing children database includes the names of the missing children along with their physical description and last known location. If your terminal has a graphics mode, you can see a portrait of this missing child.

If you have any relevant information about a missing child, please contact the detective listed for the case.

10.5.3
New Car Showroom   **NEWCAR**
New Car Showroom is a comparison shopping guide for consumers making new vehicle purchases. You can examine and compare features and specifications of passenger cars, trucks, vans and special-purpose vehicles. Over 700 foreign and domestic cars and trucks are compared in prices, standard and optional features and technical specifications, such as fuel economy and roominess.

10

10.5.4
Information USA   **INFOUSA**
Refer to 10.3.1

10.5.4.12
Electronic Answer Man   **EAM**
Refer to 10.3.1.12

10.5.5
Microsearch   **MSH**
Microsearch is a searchable database of microcomputer information. It contains over 20,000 abstracts of both product reviews from over 200+ microcomputer publications and product literature from 4,500 manufacturers/software publishers. Three categories are covered in Microsearch: Software Information, Hardware/Services Accessories Information, and the Directory of Manufacturers. Within the software and hardware information categories, Microsearch can be searched by subject, micro or operating system, product name, manufacturer, publication date or document type. Updated twice a month.

10.6
Services for Educators   **EDU-10**
This section contains information and services for educators and others interested in education.

10.6.1
Academic Am. Encyclopedia   **ENCYCLOPEDIA**
Refer to 10.2

10.6.2
The Multiple Choice   **MULTIPLECHOI**
The Multiple Choice is a collection of tests that are designed to be fun. There really is
something for everyone from kids to adults. It includes IQ tests, personality tests, trivia
questions, a test that simulates the Miller Analogies test, sports tests, and even a touch-
type tutor which provides 20 lessons for learning touch-typing on your computer at your
own pace.

10.6.4
Computer Training Forum   **DPTRAIN**
The Computer Training Forum is for computer trainers, teachers, information center staff,
vendors and anyone else with an opinion on the computer learning process. Data libraries
contain information on training techniques, office automation, careers and computers in
schools. International members contribute reports on computer trends overseas. Members
can enroll in free online Professional Seminars taught by leading instructors across the
country.

10.6.5
EPIE On-Line   **EPE**
EPIE Database offers educational consumers objective evaluations of educational products, specifically educational software and hardware. Professional advice on products'
worth and their effective use is also included in this searchable version of TESS, The Educational Software Selector. **$**

10.6.5.2
EPIE Forum **EPIEFORUM**

The EPIE Forum is dedicated to the exchange of information and ideas concerning educational courseware, products and services. News and events of interest to computer-oriented educators, students and parents are discussed. The EPIE Forum is open to everyone.

A closely related product, the EPIE Database (GO EPE), has information on educational software and hardware.

10.6.6
The Whiz Quiz **WHIZ**

Do you think you are a knowledgeable person? The Whiz Quiz sponsored by Grolier's Academic American Encyclopedia will test your knowledge in a variety of categories including geography, current events, movies, sports, music, science, literature, history and myths and legends. Up to four people can play. The top ten scores for a session will enter the Wizard Hall of Fame.

10.6.8
Peterson's College Database **PETERSON**

Peterson's College Database offers the subscriber a comprehensive database which contains detailed descriptions of over 3,000 accredited or approved U.S. and Canadian colleges that grant associate and/or bachelor degrees. Subscribers may search colleges by characteristics or college name/location. The guide will also give you in-depth information about specific aspects of any college you choose. **$**

10.6.10
AEJMC Forum **AEJMC**

The AEJMC Forum is a good source of information for journalism professionals, teachers, researchers and students. This forum is sponsored by the Association for Education in Journalism and Mass Communication. In it journalists discuss ethics and share tips for researching stories, job opening information and ideas for covering stories.

10.7
Services for the Handicapped **HANDICAPPED**

Services for the Handicapped includes a disabilities forum and a handicapped users' database.

10

10.7.1
Disabilities Forum   DISABILITIES

The Disabilities Forum is a communication facility for anyone interested in disabilities to exchange information. Disabled people share information, ideas and experiences related to their daily living. Parents and families of disabled people and professionals who work with disabled people also share their experiences and information.

The Disabilities Forum is open to everyone.

10.7.2
Handicapped Users' Database   HUD

Handicapped Users' Database provides articles and topics of interest both for and about the handicapped. Included are a reference library, lists of organizations and computer products specifically geared for use by handicapped individuals. An online message board for the exchange of ideas is also available.

10.7.2.1
National Issues/People Forum   ISSUESFORUM

The National Issues/People Forum is a forum for the free exchange of ideas about current issues and names in the news. There are sections for discussion of peace, politics, individualism, high tech, handicapped, paranormal, men and women's issues, youth and social issues. A number of regularly-scheduled conferences are held, and the data libraries contain many interesting articles, message threads and conference transcripts.

10.7.2.6
Rehabilitation Research and Development Database   REHAB

The Rehabilitation Research and Development Database carries information on rehabilitation engineering for researchers, educators, handicapped people and their families. Information sources include the *Journal of Rehabilitation Research and Development,* the *Rehabilitation Technology Transfer Exchange Newsletter,* and a current bibliography of relevant articles. Progress on ongoing research and a calendar of upcoming conferences keep members up-to- date.

10.8
Services for Students/Parents   EDU-20

This section contains those products of special interest to students and educators including college boards, travel, an encyclopedia and a guide to colleges.

10.8.1
Academic Am. Encyclopedia   ENCYCLOPEDIA
Refer to 10.2

10.8.2
The Multiple Choice
Refer to 10.6.2

MULTIPLECHOI

10.8.3
EPIE On-Line
Refer to 10.6.5

EPE

10.8.3.2
EPIE Forum
Refer to 10.6.5.2

EPIEFORUM

10.8.6
The Whiz Quiz
Refer to 10.6.6

WHIZ

10.8.7
Students' Forum

STUFO

The Student's Forum is popular with middle school students who can share their ideas and interests with other students around the country. Teachers of junior high students exchange ideas on using the forum.

10.8.8
Peterson's College Database
Refer to 10.6.8

PETERSON

10.8.9
Science/Math Education Forum

SCIENCE

This forum serves a variety of needs for Science Educators, students and others with interests in science and science education. It includes a large data library of software which can be downloaded into class and home computers.

10.9
Trivia/Thought Games

TTGAMES

These games will stretch your mind and test your knowledge.

10.9.1
Baffle

BAFFLE

Baffle enables you to test your vocabulary, learn new words, or both. The object is to form words using adjacent letters that appear on a 4 x 4 display. The trick is to find as many words as possible in three minutes. It's not as simple as you may think. As a matter of fact, it's downright BAFFLING.

10.9.2
The Multiple Choice

MULTIPLECHOI

The Multiple Choice is a collection of tests that are designed to be fun. There really is something for everyone from kids to adults. It includes IQ tests, personality tests, trivia questions, a test that simulates the Miller Analogies test, sports tests, and even a touch-type tutor which provides 20 lessons for learning touch-typing on your computer at your own pace.

10.9.2.1.4
Slogans for Sale   **SLOGANS**

This trivia game in The Multiple Choice tests your knowledge of TV advertisements. Can you fill in the missing words when given part of the slogan? A high score can put your name on the honor roll of Madison Avenue Masters.

10.9.2.1.9
Stage II — Two Stage Trivia   **STAGEII**

Refer to 10.9.5

10.9.3
Science Trivia   **SCITRIVIA**

Is there a budding Einstein in the audience? Even if you missed the Nobel Prize this year, you can challenge the top scorers in the Science Trivia Hall of Fame. Test your knowledge of biology, chemistry, physics and mathematics through the Science Trivia Quiz. The multiple choice questions are changed weekly. Questions and comments can be discussed in the Science/Math Forum (GO SCIENCE).

10.9.4
SHOWBIZQUIZ   **SHOWBIZ**

SHOWBIZQUIZ is a trivia game that tests your knowledge of the entertainment world in a variety of categories such as Frank Sinatra, the Twilight Zone or the Rolling Stones.

10.9.5
Stage II — Two Stage Trivia   **STAGEII**

Stage II is a trivia game whereby you answer three trivia questions and then look for a common theme in the answers. It can be played individually or as a group.

10.9.7
The Whiz Quiz   **WHIZ**

Do you think you are a knowledgeable person? The Whiz Quiz sponsored by Grolier's Academic American Encyclopedia will test your knowledge in a variety of categories including geography, current events, movies, sports, music, science, literature, history and myths and legends. Up to four people can play. The top ten scores for a session will enter the Wizard Hall of Fame.

10

10.9.8
Word Scramble   **SCRAMBLE**

Fi oyu acn keam nesse fo sethe dorws, ouy ilwl jneyo isth maeg.

The above sentence gives you a brief idea of how word scramble works: the computer scrambles the word and you get to unscramble it. If you score well, you may be eligible for the Hall of Fame.

You can play Word Scramble on any terminal, but the display is greatly enhanced if your communications software has cursor control capabilities.

Dogo cukl!

10.9.9
You Guessed It!   **YGI**

You Guessed It! is a real-time, multi-player game show simulation, in which players form teams and answer general information and trivia questions. There's interaction between players, as well as with a cast of "online personalities." There is a lobby for meeting other players, a BIO feature, which lets you learn more about those playing, and a post-game lounge. Will you meet new friends, have fun, and discover the True Meaning of Life? You Guessed It!

10.10
Educational Forums   **EDU-50**

This section contains educational forums dealing with educational topics including disabilities, foreign language, science and math.

10.10.1
ADCIS Forum   **ADCIS**

The Association for the Development of Computer-Based Instructional Systems is a nonprofit association dedicated to advancing the investigation and utilization of computer-based education and training. Nonmembers of the organization can review information included in this forum.

10.10.2
Disabilities Forum   **DISABILITIES**

Refer to 10.7.1

10.10.3
Computer Training Forum   **DPTRAIN**

Refer to 10.6.4

10.10.4
EPIE Forum   **EPIEFORUM**

Refer to 10.6.5.2

10.10.5
Education Forum   **EDFORUM**

The Education Forum is designed to meet the diverse needs of people involved in the teaching and learning process. This includes teachers, parents, students, faculty members and other professionals in the education field. The increasing use of microcomputers and other high technologies in our schools and homes has been a natural topic of focus of discussion in this forum.

10

10.10.6
Educational Research Forum   **EDRESEARCH**

The Education Research Forum is for people who are interested in research about the process and products of education. Through the forum, the latest research findings are shared and compared, and a dialogue is established between researchers and educators in the schools. Sponsored by the Midwestern Educational Research Association.

10.10.7
Foreign Language Education Forum   FLEFO
The Foreign Language Forum provides a service to both general and specific interests in the area of foreign languages and foreign language learning. It includes:

- Conferences
- A job bank for translators, educators and students
- Information on legislation and factors influencing the foreign language profession and
- A list of professional organizations.

10.10.8
LOGO Forum   LOGOFORUM
The Logo Forum uses a light-hearted approach to explore the use of the Logo computer language and technologies that influence our lives. Cartoon characters keep interest high.

10.10.9
Science/Math Education Forum   SCIENCE
Refer to 10.8.9

10.10.10
Students' Forum   STUFO
Refer to 10.8.7

10.10.11
Space Education Forum   SPACEED
Teachers, motivated students, and anyone interested in the development of space-related curriculums in the classroom can exchange resources and ideas in the Space Education Forum. The agenda coincides with the Teacher in Space Education Foundation, directed by NASA's Teacher in Space Program. Members can discuss topics such as the use of innovative technology in the classroom and the direction for future education in the U.S.

10.10.12
AEJMC Forum   AEJMC
Refer to 10.6.10

10

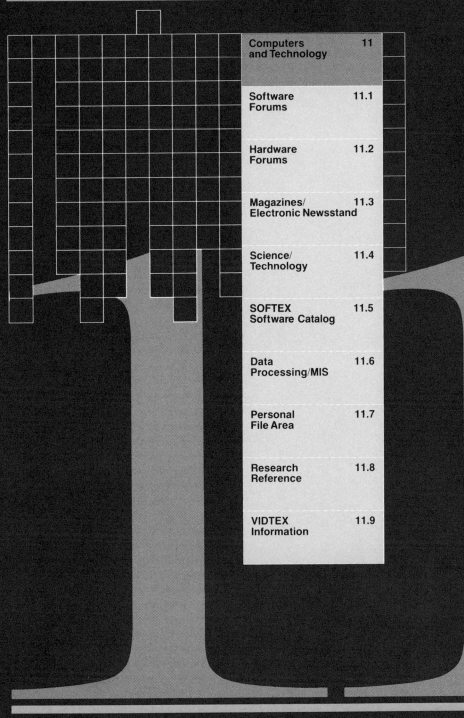

Computers and Technology	11
Software Forums	11.1
Hardware Forums	11.2
Magazines/ Electronic Newsstand	11.3
Science/ Technology	11.4
SOFTEX Software Catalog	11.5
Data Processing/MIS	11.6
Personal File Area	11.7
Research Reference	11.8
VIDTEX Information	11.9

This chapter contains all the products that have to do with computers and technology. It includes software and hardware forums, electronic magazines and newsletters.

11.1
Software Forums   SOFTWARE
Software Forums enable the users of different software packages to exchange ideas and solutions to problems. Some forums are supported by the software publishers.

11.1.1
AI EXPERT Forum   AIE
AI Expert is a forum for readers of *AI Expert Magazine* and those interested in artificial intelligence. In this forum, you can query industry and academic leaders in the AI field as well as exchange AI information with other members. As a member, you have access to public domain expert systems and software. Articles, bibliographies, news and product reviews are available in human readable form.

11

11.1.2
Aldus Forum   **ALDUS**

If you're interested in desktop publishing and Aldus Pagemaker, you'll want to join the Aldus Forum. In addition to idea exchanges with other users, detailed information on new product releases is available. Libraries contain technical support notes, templates for design formatting, and downloadable public domain and shareware programs. Aldus Forum is operated by the Aldus technical support staff who will answer your questions within 24 hours.

11.1.3
Ashton-Tate Support Library   **ASHTON**

The Ashton-Tate Support Library is an easy-to-use, menu-driven reference center and forum for users of dBase II and III, Framework and Multimate. The library is maintained by the A-T Software Support Center, which provide new product updates and announcements. The Ashton-Tate Forum (GO ASHFORUM) and monthly user surveys give members a direct line to A-T decision makers.

11.1.3.7
Ashton-Tate Forum   **ASHFORUM**

The Ashton-Tate Forum provides users of Ashton-Tate products with support from the Ashton-Tate Support Center. Subscribers can also exchange information, ideas and solutions with other Ashton-Tate users. In addition, sample programs and usage articles for each of Ashton-Tate's major products are available. You can also find information on specific problems immediately in the Ashton-Tate support library (GO ASHTON).

11.1.4
Autodesk Forum   **ADESK**

Autodesk is a computer-aided design (CAD) software forum. It offers information on Autodesk products, applications programs, usage tips and product support. Autodesk provides a worldwide meeting place for AutoCAD users, dealers, peripheral manufacturers, applications developers and Autodesk staff.

11.1.5
Borland International   **BORLAND**

The Borland International Forum enables users of Borland software to exchange information and discuss programming with other users of Borland software. Included are sections on Turbo Pascal, Sidekick and Superkey.

11

11.1.5.7
Borland Language Products Forum   **BORPRO**

If you are interested in learning more about programming with Turbo Pascal, Turbo Prolog or other Borland International products, explore the Borland Language Products Forum. In this forum, you can participate in discussions with other members concerning these products and receive help from them. You can also work with other members on joint online projects.

11.1.5.8
Borland Application Products Forum   **BROAPP**

The Borland Application Products Forum is for users of the Borland Application Products — SideKick, SuperKey, Turbo Lightning and Reflex. Members can talk to other members or ask technical questions from the Borland Technical Support Representatives. Data Libraries contain patches, enhancement programs and product information.

11.1.6
CADRE Forum   **CADRE**

The CADRE Forum is for users of Applied Data Research (ADR) products such as ROSCOE, VOLLIE, IDEAL, ETC and EMAIL. Members can have debates, exchange messages, and participate in live conferences. Bulletins keep members informed about the CADRE Forum and coming events. Data libraries contain reports, software, spreadsheets and product reviews.

11.1.7
Computer Consultant's Forum   **CONSULT**

The Computer Consultant's Forum is the place for computer consultants to exchange ideas and information on networks, product vendors, commercial software and equipment. Independent consultants can share business tips, technical information and solutions to client problems. The forum is sponsored by the Independent Computer Consultants Association (ICCA), which represents data processing professionals.

11.1.8
Computer Language Magazine   **CLM**

The Computer Language Magazine is a gathering place for professionals and serious amateurs who are fluent in two or more computer languages. Discussions center on the merits of various languages as well as topics of interest to the professional programmer. It serves as a distribution center for programs referred to in the print version of the magazine.

11

11.1.9
CP/M Forum   **CPMSIG**

The CP/M Forum is dedicated to users of the CP/M 8-bit and 16-bit computer operating systems. Subscribers exchange information and discuss problems with other CP/M users. In addition to discussing CP/M itself, programs which run on CP/M computers such as word processors and database programs are discussed.

11.1.10
Digital Research, Incorporated   **DRI**

Digital Research Forum includes Digital database and product information in addition to Digital Research news and current events. You can also find information on Digital Research dealers, warranty support and a retail price list in this section.

11.1.10.7
Digital Research Forum   **DRFORUM**

Digital Research Forum is a professional forum for Digital Research end users and software developers. Topics cover application notes and patches, concurrent operating system information and graphics. In addition, end user support and information is available.

11.1.11
Dr. Dobb's Journal Magazine   **DDJ**

In the electronic edition of Dr. Dobb's Journal, you can gather information about computer languages, tools, utilities, algorithms and programming techniques. In addition, reviews of commercial software development tools and libraries available to the professional microcomputer programmer are presented. You may also submit articles which will be reviewed for use in future publications.

11.1.12.1
Family Computing Forum   **FAMFORUM**

The Family Computing Forum members can discuss issues related to computing in the home and how it affects the family. Data libraries contain articles of special interest and members are encouraged to contribute their own.

11

11.1.12.2
Computer Club Forum   CLUB
The Computer Club Forum is a club intended for people whose computer interests are not covered by other forums. Currently, the forum attracts Adam, Timex Sinclair, Sinclair QL, Eagle IIE, Sanyo and Actrix portable computer users, although users of other computer systems are always welcome.

11.1.13
Forth Forum/Creative Solutions   FORTH
This forum is sponsored by Creative Solutions, Inc., to support its Forth products and to answer all general Forth questions. Forth is a powerful but compact programming language well-loved by programmers.

11.1.14
Javelin Forum   JAVELIN
Javelin Software's business analysis and reporting system uses a more structured approach to model building than the traditional spreadsheet. The Javelin Forum helps you take full advantage of Javelin's capabilities. These capabilities include the ability to "look behind the numbers" to determine where a specific number comes from and view problems in several ways including worksheets, formulas and presentation-quality graphs. Members of Javelin Software Corporation are online to answer your questions and provide technical support.

11.1.15
LDOS/TRSDOS6 Forum   LDOS
The LDOS/TRSDOS6 Forum welcomes all users of the Radio Shack TRS-80 Models 1, 3, 4, 4P, 40, as well as users of "work-alike" computers such as the LOBO MAX-80. Topics discussed include BASIC, "C", Fortran, Ratfor, the Z-80 assembly language and the "hardware" of the TRS-80 product line. In addition, users of TRS-80 hardware and software, the LDOS 5.1 and TRSDOS6 operating systems can gain support.

11.1.16
Living Videotext Forum   LVTFORUM
Living Videotext (LVT) is the developer and publisher of ThinkTank, Ready!, and MORE. Living Videotext Forum was established to give support to users of idea-processing software products. You can give your ideas, questions, or suggestions directly to the president of LVT.

11

11.1.17
LOGO Forum   **LOGOFORUM**

The Logo Forum uses a light-hearted approach to explore the use of the Logo computer language and technologies that influence our lives. Cartoon characters keep interest high.

11.1.18
MicroPro Forum   **MICROPRO**

The MicroPro Forum provides a medium for users of MicroPro software such as WordStar, WordStar 2000, InfoStar and CalcStar to interact with other MicroPro software users. The forum is organized into sub-topics for each of the product groups as well as a section for discussion of printers and one for Apple computers. In addition, an Add-On Products section is available where subscribers may discuss and review products developed by other companies for use with MicroPro software.

11.1.19
Microsoft Connection   **MSCON**

The Microsoft Connection is operated by the Microsoft Product Support Group for all users of their software. Members can ask questions directly to Microsoft or share information with other members. The common questions and answers section may resolve your problem on the spot. Additional features include product release announcements, training information, and a directory of Microsoft centers around the world.

11.1.19.6
Microsoft Forum   **MSOFT**

The Microsoft Users Group provides a forum where users can communicate with Microsoft, to ask questions about various Microsoft products and receive product information.

11.1.20
Monogram Software Forum   **MONOGRAM**

Users of Monogram's software products, including Dollars and Sense and Moneyline, can use this forum to exchange information and applications. The data libraries are managed by Monogram Software's technical support and analysis department. The libraries contain answers to commonly asked questions, as well as examples of stock transactions, billing applications, credit card management and payroll administration. Monogram compatibility with IBM, Apple, Macintosh and Atari is also discussed.

11

11.1.21
OS-9 Forum   OS9

The OS9 Operating System Forum is dedicated to users of the OS9 operating system. The forum contains programs, utilities, data files, hints, tips and discussions that pertain to OS9.

11.1.22
Pascal (MUSUS)   MUSUS

The Pascal (MUSUS) Forum is a membership benefit of USUS, Inc., the UCSD Pascal System User Society. Through MUSUS, members of USUS exchange information on a variety of topics, mostly centered on use of the UCSD Pascal, Apple Pascal and similar software systems.

11.1.23
Programmers' Forum   PROSIG

The Programmers Forum is for anyone who is interested in programming computers, whether beginner or expert. If it has to do with programming, it is likely that one of the members has had experience with it and can save you money, time and frustration by steering you away from a bad product or idea or towards a good one. The data libraries contain numerous programs and even computer humor.

11.1.24
Software Publishing Online   SPC

The Software Publishing Company was started by individuals who believe that busy professionals need productivity tools that are quickly learned. Thus, SPC developed a family of integrated products that stress simple functionality. Their PFS (Personal Filing System) line includes a filing system, a report writer, a word processor and planner. Their Harvard Software line consists of project management software and the Harvard Professional Publisher. Subscribers can join the Software Publishing Forum to exchange ideas on SPC products and to keep up with the latest developments.

11.1.24.5
Software Publishing Forum   SPCFORUM

The Software Publishing Forum is designed to get technical and product information to its members. The data libraries contain information on individual products as well as valuable templates to be used with PFS software.

11

11.1.25
Whole Earth Software   **WHOLEEARTH**

The Whole Earth Software Forum offers subscribers information on the best resources available for computer-oriented and non-computer-oriented purposes. Topics include reviews and recommendations of computer software, computer conferencing and telecommunications, the health hazards of computers, and the general effects of computers on people. In addition, the online publication of the Whole Earth Chronicle Column, a weekly guide to recommended tools and ideas, is included.

11.1.26
World of Lotus   **LOTUS**

The World of Lotus is sponsored and maintained by the Lotus Development Corporation to provide support to users of Lotus products and information about Lotus products and services. It includes news releases and other company information from Lotus, a list of software books and periodicals that complement Lotus products, technical product information, and answers to commonly asked questions. It provides "electronic distribution" of new device drivers, problem fixes and other technical information. Also included in the World of Lotus are the 1-2-3 Users Forum, the Symphony Users Forum, and the Jazz Users Forum all of which feature communication with Lotus product support as well as with other Lotus users.

11.1.26.6
Lotus 1-2-3 User Forum   **LOTUS123**

Lotus Development Corporation established the 1-2-3 Users Forum as part of the World of Lotus, and it is maintained by Lotus staff members. The forum provides registered members with the ability to:

- Read and leave messages to other members and to Lotus Development Corporation
- Upload and download applications software from the public domain libraries
- Share interests with other 1-2-3 members and
- Participate in online conferences.

11.1.26.7
Lotus Symphony User Forum   **SYMPHONY**

The Symphony Users Forum is similar to the 1-2-3 Users Forum except that the subject matter is geared to Lotus Symphony.

11

11.1.26.8
Graphics Products   **LOTUSGRAPHIC**
Users of Freelance, Freelance Plus and Graphwriter can exchange ideas in the Lotus
Graphics Products Forum. Members discuss graphic business communication such as
charts, diagrams, word charts, freehand drawings, symbols and maps. Data libraries
contain public domain software and symbols. A catalog of member interests and specialties can put you in touch with compatible fellow members.

11.1.26.9
Lotus Jazz Forum   **LOTUSJAZZ**
The Jazz Development Forum is the third forum in the World of Lotus. Like the 1-2-3 Users
Forum and the Symphony Users Forum, registered members can:

- Read and leave messages to other members and to the Lotus Development Corporation
- Upload and download applications software from the public domain data library
- Share interest with other 1-2-3 members and
- Participate in online conferencing.

11.2
Hardware Forums   **HARDWARE**
Hardware Forums enable users of particular hardware to exchange ideas. Many forums
include extensive data libraries, software programs and interaction with hardware
manufacturers.

11

11.2.1
Apple Users Group   MAUG

There are five forums devoted to Apple computers: the Macintosh Users Forum
(GO MACUS), the Macintosh Business Forum (GO MACBIZ), the Apple Developers Forum
(GO APPDEV), the Apple II and III Forum (GO APPLE) and Apples OnLine (GO AOL).

11.2.1.1
Macintosh Users Forum   MACUS

The Macintosh Users Forum is dedicated to users of the Macintosh line of computers, as
well as the Macintosh's predecessor, the Lisa. Here you can find excellent public domain
programs, stimulating conversation through the messaging systems, and conferences with
notable software authors and high-level Apple executives such as John Sculley, Jean-
Louis Gassee and others.

11.2.1.2
Macintosh Business Forum   MACBIZ

The MAUG Macintosh Business Forum is for Macintosh users in the business world. A
variety of subjects are discussed in this forum including productivity software, spreadsheets, databases, desktop publishing, networks and accounting.

11.2.1.3
Apple Developers Forum   APPDEV

The Apple Developers Forum is geared toward developers of software and hardware for
Apple personal computers. Members can discuss tools like languages, debuggers, editors and linkers, as well as hardware enhancements. The newsletters and tech notes provide up-to-date items on Apple products. Non-developers are welcome to join and take
advantage of the data libraries.

11.2.1.4
Maug™ Apple II and III Forum   APPLE

The MAUG™ Apple II and III Forum is devoted to people interested in the use of either of
these computers. People from all over the world exchange hints and techniques, opinions
on hardware and software, and viewpoints. The database area contains a wide selection
of software for the Apple II and III computers. There are conferences with celebrities such
as Steve Wozniak and John Dvorak as well as Apple representatives who explain new
developments.

11

11.2.1.5
Apple User Groups Forum   **APPUG**
This forum is cosponsored with Apple Computer Incorporated. This is where Apple User Groups' officers can have direct contact with Apple. Along with the officers, members of user groups can meet and exchange information and newsletters. Individuals can also use this forum to find the Apple User Group closest to them.

11.2.1.6
Apples OnLine   **AOL**
Apples OnLine is a comprehensive electronic magazine for Apple users. This magazine contains updated information on various Apple users groups, their newsletters and other Apple related magazines. Some of the users groups and magazines represented include the Berkeley Macintosh Users Group (BMUG), Washington Apple Pi (WAP), the Apple III Newsletter and the Third Apple Users Group (TAUTALES).

11.2.2
ATARI Forums   **SIGATARI**
There are three forums devoted to Atari computers: the Atari 8-Bit Forum (GO ATARI8), the Atari 16-Bit Forum (GO ATARI16), the Atari Developers Forum (GO ATARIDEV) and ANTIC ONLINE (GO ANTIC), an electronic magazine.

11.2.2.2
ATARI 8-Bit Forum   **ATARI8**
The forum is not affiliated with Atari Corporation but is maintained by independent Forum Administrators (SysOps) and centers on the Atari 8-bit computer. The data libraries contain programs, text files, help information, product reviews and transcripts of previous conferences. The Forum Administrators and others in the forum are willing to help you and answer your questions.

11.2.2.3
ATARI 16-Bit Forum   **ATARI16**
This forum is similar to the Atari 8-Bit Forum but pertains to the ST-series (16-bit) Atari computers.

11.2.2.4
ATARI Developers Forum   **ATARIDEV**
This third Atari forum supports the special interests related to the development of software and hardware development for both the 8-bit and 16-bit lines of Atari computers.

11

11.2.2.5
ANTIC ONLINE   ANTIC
ANTIC ONLINE is the first online magazine exclusively for Atari computer users. Within this magazine you will find the latest Atari news, product surveys, letters to the editor and product reviews.

11.2.3
Commodore Users Network   CBMNET
There are five forums devoted to Commodore computers: the Amiga Forum (GO AMIGAFORUM), the Commodore Arts and Games Forum (GO CBMART), the Commodore Communications Forum (GO CBMCOM), the Commodore Programming Forum (GO CBMPRG) and the Commodore Service Forum (GO CBM2000).

11.2.3.1
Amiga Forum   AMIGAFORUM
The Amiga Forum offers news, information, ideas and programs for Commodore's Amiga personal computer. Anyone is welcome to participate in the Amiga Forum — Amiga owners, software developers, prospective owners, and people who are just interested in watching the development of a new computer.

11.2.3.2
Commodore Arts and Games Forum   CBMART
Commodore Arts and Games Forum is an interactive electronic forum dedicated to the support and dissemination of news. It includes public domain games, graphics and music for the Commodore 8-bit line of computers.

11.2.3.3
Commodore Communications Forum   CBMCOM
Commodore Communications Forum is an interactive electronic forum dedicated to the support, dissemination of news, discussions of information regarding software application programs, telecommunications and user-oriented topics for the Commodore 8-bit line of computers. It includes various public domain software.

11.2.3.4
Commodore Programming Forum   CBMPRG
The Commodore Programming Forum is an interactive forum dedicated to the support, dissemination, and discussion of information regarding the programming and technical aspects of the C-128, C-64, PET, VIC-20, and B128 computers, along with various public domain programs to aid the programmer in the techniques of programming.

11

11.2.3.5
Commodore Service Forum   **CBM2000**

Commodore Service Forum is a forum for direct customer service with Commodore. There are no data libraries but there are conferencing and a message board.

11.2.4
Computer Club Forum   **CLUB**

The Computer Club Forum is a club intended for people whose computer interests are not covered by other forums. Currently, the forum attracts Adam, Timex Sinclair, Sinclair QL, Eagle IIE, Sanyo and Actrix portable computer users, although users of other computer systems are always welcome.

11.2.5
DEC Users Network   **DECUNET**

The DEC Users Network is comprised of three forums: the DEC PC Forum (GO DECPC), the PDP-11 Forum (GO PDP11) and the VAX Forum (GO VAXSIG).

11.2.5.1
DEC PC Forum   **DECPC**

The DEC PC Forum is intended for users of Digital Equipment Corp. (DEC) personal computers. Members exchange information, ideas, public domain programs, and problems concerning DEC PCs with other members.

11.2.5.2
PDP-11 Forum   **PDP11**

This forum encourages the exchange of software designed to run on Digital Equipment Corporation's PDP/LSI computer systems and covers many languages used on PDPs including Macro, Fortran, Basic, Basic-Plus, "C", DIBOL & DBL, and Pascal. PDP-11 Users Group is designed to facilitate communication between users of the PDP-11, LSI-11, and PDP-10 series of computers.

11.2.5.3
VAX Forum   **VAXSIG**

The VAX Forum enables users of Digital Equipment Corporation's line of 32-bit computers to share information and ideas with other VAX users. A section of the forum is reserved for members who use the Unix operating system.

11

11.2.6
Epson Forum   **EPSON**

EpsOnLine provides Epson microcomputer/printer users with product information, technical assistance, public domain software, and a nationwide communications network. Also included are a message exchange area, database "reference libraries", and forums which offer the Epson user valuable technical insight into the product's use.

11.2.7
Heath Users Group (HUG)   **HEATHUSERS**

Heath Users Group's purpose is to further the exchange of information about Heath/Zenith computers in order to enhance and maintain their usefulness. The forum encourages information from Heath/Zenith users regarding software/peripheral functions. In addition, the field of robotics is discussed.

11.2.8
Hewlett-Packard PC Forum   **HP**

The Hewlett-Packard PC Forum is one component of Hewlett-Packard/Online, an online information service to help you achieve the most value from Hewlett-Packard personal computers. It is supported by Hewlett-Packard, and you can converse online with HP support engineers.

11.2.9
IBM Users Network   **IBMNET**

This forum is devoted to the topic of the IBM Personal Computer and IBM PC "compatibles." It includes the IBM New Users Forum (GO IBMNEW), IBM Communications Forum (GO IBMCOM), IBM Hardware Forum (GO IBMHW), IBM Junior Forum (GO IBMJR) and IBM Software Forum (GO IBMSW).

11.2.9.1
IBM New Users Forum   **IBMNEW**

If you are just getting started with your IBM, either in the world of communications or using the CompuServe forums, you might want to drop by this forum.

11.2.9.2
IBM Communications Forum   **IBMCOM**

This forum is devoted to the topic of telecommunications on the IBM Personal Computer and compatible computers.

11

11.2.9.3
IBM Hardware Forum   IBMHW

The major theme in the IBM Hardware Forum is the discussion of the various products available for the PC. The PC world changes rapidly and keeping up to date on new developments and sharing experiences with certain products make purchasing decisions easier. In the data libraries are hardware related programs and reviews of new and useful products.

11.2.9.4
IBM Junior Forum   IBMJR

Specific needs of the PCjr are addressed in this forum. It includes information on public domain programs and information relating to common problems, solutions and experiences.

11.2.9.5
IBM Software Forum   IBMSW

This forum is devoted to the topic of software on the IBM Personal Computer and any and all other compatible computers.

11.2.9.6
PC Vendor Support Forum   PCVEN

The PC Vendor Support Forum provides subscribers with support from multiple vendors of PC products. The vendors include ButtonWare (PC-File+, word processing, graphics and communication), Mansfield Software (KEDIT and REXX), the Software Group (Enable) and Broderbund (entertainment and productivity software).

11.2.10
Kaypro Users' Group   KAYPRO

Kaypro Forum enables Kaypro users to exchange information and assistance with other Kaypro users. There are 10 message areas and databases including information on products which can be added to Kaypro computers, hardware related files, and Help files which are designed to get the novice user off on the right foot.

11

11.2.11
Tandy Users Network   **TANDYNET**

The Tandy Users Network comprises eight Tandy product forums: the Color Computer Forum (GO COCO), the LDOS/TRSDOS6 Forum (GO LDOS), the Model 100/Portables Forum (GO M100SIG), the OS-9 Forum (GO OS9), the Tandy Professional Forum (GO TRS80PRO), the TANGENT Forum (GO TANGENT) and the Tandy Corporation Newsletter (GO TRS).

11.2.11.1
Color Computer Forum   **COCO**

The TRS-80 CoCo Users Group provides independent support for owners and operators of the TRS-80 Color Computer and related peripherals. Technical information, programming examples, and a forum where CoCo owners can meet and discuss problems and desires are also included.

11.2.11.2
LDOS/TRSDOS6 Forum   **LDOS**

The LDOS/TRSDOS6 Forum welcomes all users of the Radio Shack TRS-80 Models 1, 3, 4, 4P, 40, as well as users of "work-alike" computers such as the LOBO MAX-80. Topics discussed include BASIC, "C", Fortran, Ratfor, the Z-80 assembly language and the "hardware" of the TRS-80 product line. In addition, users of TRS-80 hardware and software, the LDOS 5.1 and TRSDOS6 operating systems can gain support.

11.2.11.3
Model 100 Forum   **M100SIG**

The Model 100 Forum is intended for the users of the TRS-80 Model 100. Subscribers can share knowledge, experiences, programs, and product information with other subscribers. There are 10 message board topics and databases which contain 1,000+ files of interest to Model 100 users. The data library and message board also support the Tandy 200 and NEC 8201A.

11.2.11.4
OS-9 Forum   **OS9**

The OS9 Operating System Forum is dedicated to users of the OS9 operating system. The forum contains programs, utilities, data files, hints, tips and discussions that pertain to OS9.

11

11.2.11.5
Tandy Professional Forum   **TRS80PRO**

The Tandy Professional Forum offers Tandy computer users an avenue for exchange of information with other subscribers regarding the full line of Tandy computers.

11.2.11.6
TANGENT Forum   **TANGENT**

TANGENT is the forum for business users of Tandy computers. Members have access to up-to-date technical information, support and input. You can keep informed through bulletins, public message boards, conferences and member discussions. Data libraries contain downloadable public domain software, product reviews, reports and journal abstracts. The emphasis in this forum is on the Tandy Model 2/12/16/600 line of equipment but, of course, everyone is welcome.

11.2.11.7
Tandy Corporation Newsletter   **TRS**

Tandy Newsletter is designed to keep Tandy computer users informed of current activities within the Tandy corporation. In addition, you have access to a conference schedule and Tandy product and technical information.

11.2.12
Telecommunications Forum   **TELECOMM**

The Telecommunications Forum is dedicated to microcomputer telecommunications. Subjects under discussion include BBSing, downloading from CompuServe, terminal software, packet networks, and micro-to-mainframe links. Subscribers may also refer to the Telecommunications Forum when seeking information about problems regarding a particular modem or information service.

11.2.13
Texas Instruments News   **TINEWS**

Texas Instruments News is a menu-driven, text area where complete forum instructions, help with tricky file transfers, the latest forum news, and forum feedback can be found.

11

11.2.13.5
Texas Instruments Forum   **TIFORUM**

The Texas Instruments Forum is for anyone interested in any model of Texas Instruments brand computers especially the TI-99/4A and TI Professional. The TI Forum has an active message base and rapidly expanding data libraries. Weekly conferences are also scheduled.

Members and Forum Administrators (SysOps) will be happy to assist new subscribers. The TI Forum is now a major source of TI information across the country, supplementing a local users group network and bulletin board systems.

11.3
Magazines/Electronic Newsstand   **MAGAZINES**

This electronic magazine rack includes electronic versions of several print magazines as well as newsletters and magazines which do not have a corresponding print version.

11.3.1
AI EXPERT Magazine   **AIE**
Refer to 11.1.1

11.3.2
ANTIC ONLINE   **ANTIC**
Refer to 11.2.2.5

11.3.3
Apples OnLine   **AOL**
Refer to 11.2.1.6

11.3.4
Commodore Information Network   **CBM**
The Commodore Information Network contains information relevant to Commodore computer users and gives you a place to meet other subscribers to exchange ideas and information.

11.3.5
Computer Language Magazine   **CLM**
Refer to 11.1.8

11.3.6
Digital Research, Incorporated   **DRI**
Refer to 11.1.10

11.3.6.7
Digital Research Forum   **DRFORUM**
Refer to 11.1.7

11.3.7
Dr. Dobb's Journal   **DDJ**
Refer to 11.1.1

11

11.3.8
Media/Electronic Publishing   **PCS-100**

These forums are for people who are interested in communications — written, broadcast and electronic.

11.3.8.1
AI EXPERT Magazine   **AIE**

Refer to 11.3.1

11.3.8.2
Broadcast Professional Forum   **BPFORUM**

Broadcast Professional Forum covers the major publications, manufacturers and trade associations, conventions, organizations, and seminars which relate to the fields of broadcast and audio engineering, production, and land mobile communications. Also included is the latest FCC news as it relates to the broadcast and communications professions.

11.3.8.3
Computer Language Magazine   **CLM**

Refer to 11.3.5

11.3.8.4
Dr. Dobb's Journal Forum   **DDJFORUM**

Refer to 11.3.7

11.3.8.5.1
Family Computing Forum   **FAMFORUM**

Refer to 11.1.12.1

11.3.8.5.2
Computer Club Forum   **CLUB**

Refer to 11.1.12.2

11

11.3.8.6
Journalism Forum   **JFORUM**

Journalism Forum serves the professional journalist with a variety of services and specialized data libraries. Journalism Forum offers separate data libraries for Radio, TV, Print and Photo/Video Journalists. In addition, there are data libraries dedicated to jobs listings, freelance opportunities, equipment exchanges, commentary, and a listing of names and phone numbers of proven resources.

11.3.9
Family Computing Forum   **FAMFORUM**
Refer to 11.3.8.5.1

11.3.10
Microsearch   **MSH**

Microsearch is a searchable database of microcomputer information. It contains over 20,000 abstracts of both product reviews from over 200+ microcomputer publications and product literature from 4,500 manufacturers/software publishers. Three categories are covered in Microsearch: Software Information, Hardware/Services Accessories Information, and the Directory of Manufacturers. Within the software and hardware information categories, Microsearch can be searched by subject, micro or operating system, product name, manufacturer, publication date or document type. Updated twice a month.

11.3.11
Online Today   **OLT**

The Electronic Edition of CompuServe's *Online Today* magazine. The *Online Today Electronic Edition* provides daily updated computer and information industry news, CompuServe news, product announcements, reviews of new hardware, software, books and more.

11.3.11.7
Online Today Online Inquiry   **OLI**

You can request general information about an ad displayed in *Online Today* and request product literature directly from advertisers.

11.3.12
Tandy Newsletter   **TRS**
Refer to 11.3.6.11.7

11

11.4
Science/Technology Forums   **PCS-40**
These forums are for people interested in ham radio, space, electronics, and science fiction.

11.4.1
Astronomy Forum   **ASTROFORUM**
Amateur or professional stargazers can join cosmic forces with fellow astronomers from around the world. Beginners with a universe of questions can learn about hardware or techniques. Professionals can take advantage of the Astronomy Forum to rapidly disseminate information among colleges. Members of all levels can learn about national or international special events of interest. Archives contain public domain astronomy software and quality reference articles.

11.4.3
Computer Training Forum   **DPTRAIN**
The Computer Training Forum is for computer trainers, teachers, information center staff, vendors and anyone else with an opinion on the computer learning process. Data libraries contain information on training techniques, office automation, careers and computers in schools. International members contribute reports on computer trends overseas. Members can enroll in free online Professional Seminars taught by leading instructors across the country.

11

11.4.4
Consumer Electronics Forum   CEFORUM

The Consumer Electronics Forum is dedicated to exchanging information about electronic consumer products such as VCRs, telephone answering machines, compact disk players, and even earth station equipment. The forum features articles, reviews, new products and news in its data libraries. You can get answers for your questions and discuss the latest issues facing this industry. Special interactive online conferences feature guests from manufacturers such as Sony, Pioneer and Panasonic.

11.4.5
HamNet Online   HAM

HamNet Online is dedicated to serving the needs of amateur radio and short-wave listening (SWL) enthusiasts. You will find:

- Information on getting started in ham radio and SWL,
- The latest news and information on ham radio and SWL events,
- Regular "electronic editions" of amateur radio and SWL newsletters and
- Information on new technical developments.

11.4.5.3
HamNet (Ham Radio) Forum   HAMNET

This is the conferencing facility of HamNet Online and is where you can converse with others who are interested in amateur radio and short wave listening.

11.4.7
Photography Forum   PHOTOFORUM

Shutterbugs of all levels, professional and amateur, can meet in the Photography Forum. Members can discuss photography equipment, film types and camera techniques. Professionals can communicate with others in the business and share money-making ideas.

11.4.8
Picture Support Forum   PICS

The Picture Support Forum is dedicated to expanding the availability of online graphics. This forum is for exchange of information on how to create and upload graphics files, to provide graphics files for those without the ability to create them, and to maintain a display area of graphics files for downloading. Members can share information about their techniques, tips and traps.

11

11.4.9
Sci-Fi/Fantasy   **SCI**

Sci-Fi and Fantasy's forum serves the needs of people who are interested in science fiction and fantasy. You will find:

- The Science Fiction and Fantasy Forum (GO SCI-FI),
- The Comic Book Forum (GO COMIC),
- News about publishing, movie making, TV, conventions and
- Book reviews and commentaries.

11.4.9.1
Sci-Fi/Fantasy Forum   **SCI-FI**

The Sci-Fi Forum is a place where people who enjoy Science Fiction can get together and chat about their mutual likes and dislikes. There are also conferences with famous authors, producers and publishers.

11.4.9.2
Comic Book Forum   **COMIC**

This forum features news, reviews and conferences with some of the greats of comic books and animations.

11.4.10
Science/Math Education Forum   **SCIENCE**

This forum serves a variety of needs for Science Educators, students and others with interests in science and science education. It includes a large data library of software which can be downloaded into class and home computers.

11.4.11
Space Education Forum   **SPACEED**

Teachers, motivated students, and anyone interested in the development of space-related curriculums in the classroom can exchange resources and ideas in the Space Education Forum. The agenda coincides with the Teacher in Space Education Foundation, directed by NASA's Teacher in Space Program. Members can discuss topics such as the use of innovative technology in the classroom and the direction for future education in the U.S.

11.4.12
Space Forum   **SPACEFORUM**

Space Forum is for subscribers interested in all aspects of space exploration, travel, research, colonization, research and development, and related activities. NASA news releases are posted regularly in this forum.

11.5
CompuServe's SOFTEX^{SM} Software Catalog   **SOFTEX**

CompuServe's SOFTEX^{SM} is an electronic software catalog which enables you to purchase and receive commercial software through your personal computer without the inconvenience of driving to a computer store or waiting for mail delivery. SOFTEX's growing selection includes popular commercially-available software as well as hard-to-find software from smaller vendors. Selections include programming utilities, tutorials, spreadsheets, accounting packages and games for most personal computers.

Your machine requires terminal software that supports an error-checking file transfer protocol, such as XMODEM or CompuServe's "B" protocol. Purchases are billed to your CompuServe account.

11.6
Data Processing/MIS   **DPMIS**

This area contains forums, databases and news products concerned with processing and transmitting information via computers.

11.6.1
CADRE Forum   **CADRE**

Refer to 11.1.6

11.6.2
PR and Marketing Forum   **PRSIG**

The Public Relations and Marketing Forum provides a special interest group for professional communicators such as public relations, marketing and communications directors or those holding related jobs in the public and private sector. The data libraries cover a wide variety of topics as they relate to PR including government, education, public affairs, financial institutions, consumer affairs, computers, high tech, health/social services and PRSA. The teleconferences enable a member to hear from recognized communications experts. In addition, the forum may be used to establish meetings by members for specific reasons.

11

11.6.3
Computer Consultant's Forum   **CONSULT**
Refer to 11.1.7

11.6.4
Microsearch   **MSH**
Refer to 11.3.10

11.6.6
IQuest   **IQU**
IQuest, CompuServe's online information retrieval service, provides easy access to more than 800 databases from companies such as Dialogue, BRS, NewsNet, Vu/text and ADP. All types of information are included. From scholarly to popular press, business-related to the obscure, IQuest is the most comprehensive source of online information anywhere.

IQuest contains fully indexed historical data and is updated electronically each day. Both bibliographic and full-text documents are available. Source materials include magazines, newspapers, indexes, conference proceedings, directories, books, newsletters, government documents, dissertations, encyclopedias, patent records and reference guides.

All IQuest databases are accessible via the same easy-to-use, menu-driven format. No training is required. IQuest offers two simple ways to retrieve information:

- IQuest-I will choose the appropriate database once a subscriber has selected a topic and
- IQuest-II allows a subscriber to go directly to a specified database.

Free, online, real-time help is available in IQuest by typing SOS. **$**

11.6.7
Computer Training Forum   **DPTRAIN**
Refer to 11.4.3

11.7
Personal File Area   **PER**
As a CompuServe subscriber you are able to store files on CompuServe. This menu choice enables you to catalog those files, edit them, rename them, change their protection level, or delete them.

You can also obtain a hard-copy printout of your files. There is an additional charge for printing. In addition, you can upload and download files, and enter the command mode. Please read your Users Guide before using the command mode. **$***

11

11.8
Research/Reference   **PCS-50**
Research/Reference contains online tutorials and information about some CompuServe software programs as well as other products which relate to microcomputers.

11.8.1
VIDTEX Information   **VID**
VIDTEX is a series of terminal emulation programs which enables the subscriber's computer to communicate with a host computer system. Some capabilities the programs provide include: RAM buffer controls, function keys, printer control, send ahead pages, and error free file transfer. VIDTEX can run on Apple, Commodore 64, IBM PC, XT, and PCjr, TRS-80 Color Computer, TRS-80 Model III and the NEW Atari VIDTEX.

11.8.2
Computer Consultant's Forum   **CONSULT**
Refer to 11.1.7

11.8.4
Text Editors/Word Processors   **PCS-121**
Text Editors/Word Processors instructs you in how to use EDIT and the ICS Editor. EDIT is used to create and edit files which you can then store in your Personal File Area.

11.8.5
Microsearch   **MSH**
Refer to 11.3.10

11.8.6
IQuest   **IQU**
Refer to 11.6.6

11.8.7
Information USA   **INFOUSA**
Information USA tells you how to use the free or nearly free government publications and services that are available. It explains the art of obtaining information from bureaucrats and gives other helpful information when dealing with the government. Information USA was extracted from the reference book of the same name written by Matthew Lesko.

11

11.8.7.12
Electronic Answer Man   **EAM**

Do you want to study overseas? How do you patent your invention? Are pests destroying your organic garden? The Electronic Answer Man can help you on almost any topic. EAM describes government publications, public agency departments, and funding sources.

11.8.8
Computer Training Forum   **DPTRAIN**

Refer to 11.4.3

11.9
VIDTEX Information   **VID**

Refer to 11.8.1

11

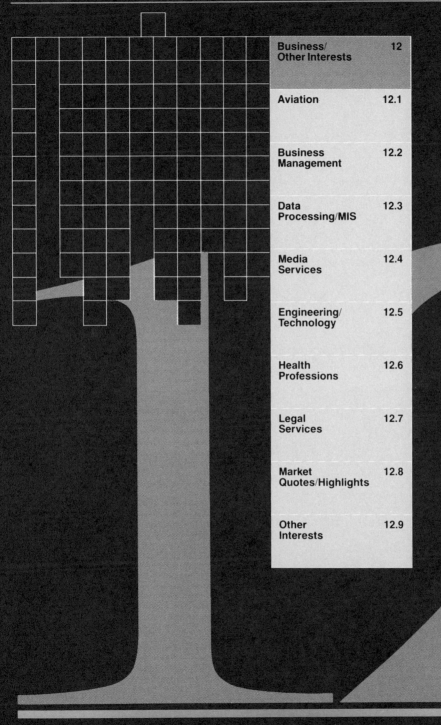

Business/Other Interests	12
Aviation	12.1
Business Management	12.2
Data Processing/MIS	12.3
Media Services	12.4
Engineering/Technology	12.5
Health Professions	12.6
Legal Services	12.7
Market Quotes/Highlights	12.8
Other Interests	12.9

This chapter covers all the interests of business, from aviation and business management through legal services and real estate. If you run a small business or a large one, this chapter holds the products to help you make good business decisions.

12.1
Aviation   **AVIATION**

This section includes material on flight planning, weather briefing, airport reviews and safety tips.

12.1.1
Aviation Safety Institute   **ASI**

Aviation Safety Institute provides information on a variety of safety-related topics. Topics include Service Difficulty Reports and Hazard Reports, along with articles on flight operations, human factors, airport reviews and safety tips. The information in ASI Monitor, an online newsletter, is updated monthly.

12.1.2
Aviation Weather   **AWX**

CompuServe Aviation Weather is instant weather for pilots. It uses the N.O.A.A. Service "A" weather wire. This is the same data used in International Flight Service stations. Most of the data is coded but is easy to read with a little practice. It includes hourly reports, terminal forecasts, NOTAMS, PIREPS, SIGMETS, AIRMETS, area forecasts and radar summaries. Updated continuously. **$**

12

12.1.3
EMI Aviation Services   **EMI**
Each of the EMI Aerodata flight planning programs produces a complete flight log for flights between any two points in the continental U.S. in a form suitable for en route navigation. EMI makes available weather briefing, trip time and distance, and a radar map.
     For radar weather you need a screen that is at least 80 characters wide. **$**

12.1.4
Aviation Forum   **AVSIG**
The Aviation Special Interest Forum is a group of people interested in computers and airplanes. It covers general flying issues, safety, weather, air traffic control, balloons and soaring, want ads and personal computer programs. AVSIG is open to any and all who care to visit and share their ideas and experience in the field of aviation.

12.1.5
Air Information/Reservations   **FLIGHTS**
Air Information/Reservations contains the Official Airline Guide Electronic Edition and Travelshopper. Both offer complete schedule and fare information for all commercial flights throughout the world. When using either of these products, you will be asked for your departure and destination cities and your date of travel. Both offer reservations and ticketing options.

12.1.5.1
OAG Electronic Edition   **OAG**
The Official Airline Guide Electronic Edition contains the schedules and availability for all commercial flights operating throughout the world. It contains fares for all North American and international flights. You can make reservations online and, depending on the airline, can select from several available ticketing options. Information on hotels and motels throughout the world is now available. Updated continually. **$**.

12.1.5.2
Travelshopper   **TWA**
Travelshopper gives direct access to the PARS reservation system. You can look up flight availability and fares for any airline in the world. It will select flights that are closest to the travel date and time that you specify. You can make reservations online. Actual ticketing must be done through your travel agent or local airlines. Additional services and travel information are provided in Travelshopper such as weather, theater information, ski conditions and in-flight meals and movies. Updated continually.

12

12.1.6
VIDTEX Weather Maps   **MAPS**
These weather maps can be displayed on most computers running CompuServe's VIDTEX terminal software or using one of the free public-domain graphics decoders from the Aviation Forum. They include a national map, surface synoptic map and an aviation weather depiction chart. These maps are black and white only. **$**

12.1.8
ModelNet   **MODELNET**
The Model Aviation Forum is a forum for the model hobbyist. Builders of model railroads, airplanes, cars and boats will find all these disciplines covered in the forum. In addition, forum members have access to newsletters and articles from "Model Aviation Magazine" and a complete contest calendar. A "Swap Shop" enables hobbyists to trade parts.

12.2
Business Management   **MANAGEMENT**
This section covers the needs of managers of both large and small businesses.

12.2.2
PR and Marketing Forum   **PRSIG**
The Public Relations and Marketing Forum provides a special interest group for professional communicators such as public relations, marketing and communications directors or those holding related jobs in the public and private sector. The data libraries cover a wide variety of topics as they relate to PR including government, education, public affairs, financial institutions, consumer affairs, computers, high tech, health/social services and PRSA. The teleconferences enable a member to hear from recognized communications experts. In addition, the forum may be used to establish meetings by members for specific reasons.

12.2.3
Int'l Entrepreneurs Network   **USEN**
The Int'l Entrepreneurs Network is an information exchange for entrepreneurs and business resources. Topics discussed include business start up procedures and the development of entrepreneurship. Members are encouraged to discuss business related problems, ideas and techniques.

12

12.2.4
DR. JOB   DRJ
DR. JOB is a weekly Questions and Answers column covering career and employment issues. Topics discussed range from corporate politics to communication to career decisions. Questions are answered either in future columns or privately via EasyPlex. In addition, a section on career tips presents valuable insight into business etiquette and current career opportunities.

12.2.6
IQuest   IQU
IQuest, CompuServe's online information retrieval service, provides easy access to more than 800 databases from companies such as Dialogue, BRS, NewsNet, Vu/text and ADP. All types of information are included. From scholarly to popular press, business-related to the obscure, IQuest is the most comprehensive source of online information anywhere.

IQuest contains fully indexed historical data and is updated electronically each day. Both bibliographic and full-text documents are available. Source materials include magazines, newspapers, indexes, conference proceedings, directories, books, newsletters, government documents, dissertations, encyclopedias, patent records and reference guides.

All IQuest databases are accessible via the same easy-to-use, menu-driven format. No training is required. IQuest offers two simple ways to retrieve information:

- IQuest-I will choose the appropriate database once a subscriber has selected a topic and
- IQuest-II allows a subscriber to go directly to a specified database.

Free, online, real-time help is available in IQuest by typing SOS. **$**

12.2.7
Information USA   INFOUSA
Information USA tells you how to use the free or nearly free government publications and services that are available. It explains the art of obtaining information from bureaucrats and gives other helpful information when dealing with the government. Information USA was extracted from the reference book of the same name written by Matthew Lesko.

12.2.7.12
Electronic Answer Man   EAM
Do you want to study overseas? How do you patent your invention? Are pests destroying your organic garden? The Electronic Answer Man can help you on almost any topic. EAM describes government publications, public agency departments and funding sources.

12

12.2.8
Computer Training Forum   **DPTRAIN**
The Computer Training Forum is for computer trainers, teachers, information center staff, vendors, and anyone else with an opinion on the computer learning process. Data libraries contain information on training techniques, office automation, careers and computers in schools. International members contribute reports on computer trends overseas. Members can enroll in free online Professional Seminars taught by leading instructors across the country.

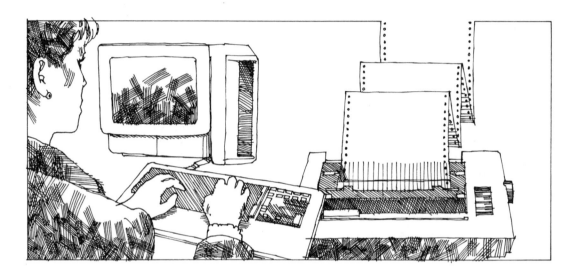

12.3
Data Processing/MIS   **DPMIS**
This area contains forums, databases and news products concerned with processing and transmitting information via computers.

12.3.1
CADRE Forum   **CADRE**
The CADRE Forum is for users of Applied Data Research (ADR) products such as ROSCOE, VOLLIE, IDEAL, ETC and EMAIL. Members can have debates, exchange messages, and participate in live conferences. Bulletins keep members informed about the CADRE Forum and coming events. Data libraries contain reports, software, spreadsheets and product reviews.

12

12.3.2
PR and Marketing Forum   **PRSIG**
Refer to 12.2.2

12.3.3
Computer Consultant's Forum   **CONSULT**
The Computer Consultant's Forum is the place for computer consultants to exchange ideas and information on networks, product vendors, commercial software and equipment. Independent consultants can share business tips, technical information and solutions to client problems. The forum is sponsored by the Independent Computer Consultants Association (ICCA), which represents data processing professionals.

12.3.4
Microsearch   **MSH**
Microsearch is a searchable database of microcomputer information. It contains over 20,000 abstracts of both product reviews from over 200+ microcomputer publications and product literature from 4,500 manufacturers/software publishers. Three categories are covered in Microsearch: Software Information, Hardware/Services Accessories Information and the Directory of Manufacturers. Within the software and hardware information categories, Microsearch can be searched by subject, micro or operating system, product name, manufacturer, publication date or document type. Updated twice a month.

12.3.6
IQuest   **IQU**
Refer to 12.2.6

12.3.7
Computer Training Forum   **DPTRAIN**
Refer to 12.2.8

12.4
Media Services   **MEDIA**
This section contains the services for people in media including broadcasting, marketing and engineering.

12

12.4.1
Broadcast Professional Forum   **BPFORUM**

Broadcast Professional Forum covers the major publications, manufacturers and trade associations, conventions, organizations and seminars which relate to the fields of broadcast and audio engineering, production and land mobile communications. Also included is the latest FCC news as it relates to the broadcast and communications professions.

12.4.2
PR and Marketing Forum   **PRSIG**

Refer to 12.2.2

12.4.4
Journalism Forum   **JFORUM**

Journalism Forum serves the professional journalist with a variety of services and specialized data libraries. Journalism Forum offers separate data libraries for Radio, TV, Print and Photo/Video Journalists. In addition, there are data libraries dedicated to jobs listings, freelance opportunities, equipment exchanges, commentary, and a listing of names and phone numbers of proven resources.

12.4.5
INCUE Online   **INCUE**

INCUE Online covers Radio and Television Broadcast Engineering, Production, Programming and Promotion. You can learn of the latest television, radio and land mobile news from InCue OnLine, an online publication. In addition, INCUE offers reviews, article summaries and previews, product announcements and FCC information. A Broadcast Professional Forum as well as a reference library also is available.

12.5
Engineering/Technology   **ENGINEERING**

This section contains those products dealing with engineering, safety and computer technology including the rapidly growing field of CAD/CAM.

12.5.1
Autodesk Forum   **ADESK**

Autodesk is a computer-aided design (CAD) software forum. It offers information on Autodesk products, applications programs, usage tips, and product support. Autodesk provides a worldwide meeting place for AutoCAD users, dealers, peripheral manufacturers, applications developers and Autodesk staff.

12

12.5.2
Broadcast Professional Forum   **BPFORUM**
Refer to 12.4.1

12.5.3
Safetynet   **SAFETYNET**
The Safetynet Forum provides an area where anyone interested in safety-related issues can post messages, participate in teleconferencing, and receive information from the data libraries. Topics covered include regulations and standards, chemical and physical hazards, hazardous materials, fire services/prevention/investigation and emergency medical services.

12.5.4
News-a-tron Market Reports   **NAT**
Market Reports gives analysis and information on petroleum, metals, currency, Foreign Exchange prices, credit markets, domestic and international interest rates, grain reports and current quotes. See Appendixes E, G and H for lists of symbols used in this product. **$**

12.5.5
INCUE Online   **INCUE**
Refer to 12.4.5

12.5.7
IQuest   **IQU**
Refer to 12.2.6

12.6
Health Professions   **MEDICAL**
Many of the products relating to health services are sponsored by professional organizations and have extensive databases. Forums offer opportunities for professionals to share the latest information on medical conditions and other health-related topics.

12.6.1
AAMSI Medical Forum   **MEDSIG**
AAMSI is sponsored by the American Association for Medical Systems and Informatics. Members represent all segments of the professional medical community and use this forum to exchange ideas and information on medically-related topics.

12

12.6.4
HealthNet   **HNT**
HealthNet is a comprehensive online medical reference source. It contains a reference library, a bimonthly newsletter and a subscriber inquiry forum. Also included is a section on sports medicine with information on nutrition, exercise and the benefits of and injuries incurred from some specific sports.

    HealthNet is updated continuously by a team of licensed, board-certified physicians.

12.6.5
Healthcom/Health Forum   **HCM**
Healthcom/Health Forum allows a subscriber to discuss health-related matters with other subscribers including topics on mental health, child care and sexuality. Subscribers also have access to biomedical literature through MEDLINE as well as current and accurate information on rare disorders and diseases through the NORD Services/Rare Disease Database. In addition, an AIDS quiz and AIDS reference library are available.

12

12.6.6
NORD Services/Rare Disease Database   NORD
The NORD Services/Rare Disease Database provides the subscriber with current and accurate information on rare disorders and diseases. Some topics covered include AIDS research, education for handicapped children, and information on digestive disease research centers. Subscribers also have access to biomedical literature through MEDLINE, and can communicate with other subscribers on various subjects. In addition, a NORD newsletter is available which explains NORD and presents news on the latest rare disease updates and facts.

12.6.7
PaperChase (MEDLINE)   PCH
PaperChase gives access to MEDLINE, the National Library of Medicine's database of references to biomedical literature. Included are over 5 million references from 3,400 journals which date from January 1966 through the current date. **$***

12.7
Legal Services   LEGAL
Legal Services include a forum and continuing education information.

12.7.1
Legal Forum   LAWSIG
The Legal Forum is designed specifically for attorneys, police, corrections officers, paralegals and laypersons interested in the law. Topics such as copyrights, bankruptcy, software/hardware for the law office, Lexis vs Westlaw, pros and cons of polygraph tests, fingerprinting children and other law-related subjects are debated.

12.7.3
IQuest   IQU
Refer to 12.2.6

12.7.4
Computer Training Forum   DPTRAIN
Refer to 12.2.8

12

12.8
Market Quotes/Highlights   **QUOTES**

This menu delivers CompuServe's MicroQuote II via menus. Experienced subscribers of these services may wish to access this service in command mode (GO MQUOTE).

The MicroQuote database contains current and historical information on more than 90,000 stocks, bonds, mutual funds and options as well as foreign exchange rates and hundreds of market indexes. Dividend, interest, distribution and split histories go back to 1968 and daily price and volume data are available back to 1974 for selected issues. MicroQuote II also contains investment data on earnings, risk and capitalization.

MicroQuote II current stock quotes are delayed approximately 20 minutes. Most commodities data are available by 6:00 p.m. Eastern Time, and price and volume information for all securities is updated and available by 8:00 a.m. the next morning.

CompuServe is very careful about the accuracy of its MicroQuote II data. We perform automated reasonability tests and use independent sources to check any discrepancies. Many major investment banking firms regularly depend upon this data.

Here are a few tips that you may find useful when using MicroQuote II:

- For stock information you will need to enter a ticker symbol or the first six digits of a CUSIP. If you do not know either of these, you can look them up using the Issue/Symbol Lookup programs, GO SYMBOLS.

- If you are at a prompt for company name or ticker symbol and you wish to exit the program, the navigational commands such as TOP or MENU will not work. Instead you need to enter /T or /M so that the system knows you are not trying to enter a company name or ticker symbol.

- For some products you will need to enter the date or the number of days, weeks or months for which you wish pricing information. Dates may be entered in several formats including mm/dd/yy (i.e. 10/15/87 or 2/7/86).

- Codes for popular Mutual funds, market indicators, stocks, exchange rates and commodities are listed in the Appendix.

12

12.8.1
Current Quotes   QQUOTE

Quick Quote, CompuServe's current quotations service includes information from national and regional exchanges and the OTC national market on over 9,000 stocks. Quotes are delayed 20 minutes, which is as soon as the exchanges will allow you to receive them without the payment of a monthly fee. The information includes volume, high, low, last, change and time of last trade or quote.

You can retrieve the quotes by specifying a ticker symbol, CUSIP, the company name or a previously stored file of ticker symbols. Optionally, retrieved data may be directed to an output file in formats readable by microcomputer spreadsheet packages. See Appendixes D and F for lists of symbols used in this product. Updated continually. **$**

12.8.2
Historical Stock/Fund Pricing   SECURITIES

This menu accesses the historical part of the MicroQuote II database in a variety of ways.

12.8.2.1
Pricing History — 1 Issue   PRICES

Pricing History — 1 Issue gives historical prices by day, week or month. It includes CUSIP, exchange code, volume, high/ask, low/bid and close/average for a given security. You may designate the beginning and ending date or a number of time periods prior to the most recent quote. See Appendixes D, E, F, G and H for lists of symbols used in this product.
Updated daily. **$**

12.8.2.2
Multiple Issues — 1 Day   QSHEET

Multiple Issues — 1 Day gives volume, close/average, high/ask, low/bid and CUSIP numbers for several issues for a given day. You may enter a previously stored file of up to 500 ticker symbols for processing. See Appendixes D, E, F, G and H for lists of symbols used in this product.
Updated daily. **$**

12.8.2.3
Price/Volume Graph   TREND

Price/Volume charting provides graphic presentations of both the traded price and the trading volume for the requested days, weeks, or months. Relevant information such as the current earnings, price, dividend, and risk information for common stocks and other securities is displayed with the graph. The program works with CompuServe's VIDTEX software or NAPLPS hardware. Your personal computer must be able to support graphics to use this product. See Appendixes D, E, F, G and H for lists of symbols used in this product. **$**

12.8.2.4
Dividends, Splits, Bond Interest   DIVIDENDS

Dividends, Splits, Bond Interest gives dividend, split and bond interest information for an issue over a given period. Hard-to-obtain mutual fund distributions are also available. You may specify the number of dividends you wish to view. The report includes the ex-date, record date, payment date, distribution type and the rate or amount of each distribution. See Appendixes D and F for lists of symbols used in this product.
    Updated daily. **$**

12.8.2.5
Pricing Statistics   PRISTATS

Pricing History Summarized provides a snapshot of price and volume performance for a requested issue over a given period. It indicates such items as whether an issue is trading closer to recent high or low prices. The statistics include the current high/ask, low/bid, and close average as well as the highest high, the highest close, the lowest low, the lowest close, the highest volume, the lowest volume, and the average and standard deviation for high, low, close, and volume. Also included are the total volume, the beta factor and the beta centile rank. See Appendixes D, E, F, G and H for lists of symbols used in this product.
    Updated daily. **$**

12.8.2.6
Detailed Issue Examination   EXAMINE

Detailed Issue Examination gives a detailed description of a single issue including trading status, recent price, dividends, risk measures and capitalization. For stocks, it shows the shares outstanding, twelve-month earnings-per-share, beta factor, indicated annual dividend and the dividend yield. For bonds, the program includes the maturity date, bond rate, yield to maturity, interest payment history and amount outstanding. Options information includes shares per contract, open interest, expiration date and exercise price. A 52-week high and low price are included for all securities. See Appendixes D, E, F, G and H for lists of symbols used in this product. **$**

12.8.2.7
Options Profile   OPRICE

Options Profile lists all options currently trading on a given common stock or market index. Coverage includes over 10,000 put and call options trading on major US and Canadian exchanges. It lists the name, closing price, pricing date, ticker symbol and exchange code for the underlying company. The exercise price and closing option price are displayed for each active option. See Appendixes E and F for lists of symbols used in this product.
    Updated daily. **$**

12

12.8.2.8
Instructions/Fees **MQP**

This section gives instructions on how to use Pricing History (GO PRICES), Multiple Issues (GO QSHEET) and Price/Volume Graph (GO TREND).

12.8.3
Highlights — Previous Day **MARKET**

Market Highlights analyzes the most recent trading day for the New York Stock Exchange, American Stock Exchange, and Over-The-Counter markets and prepares 19 different reports. Included are the most active stocks, the largest gainers and losers, stocks for which the price has risen or dropped over the past three, four, or five trading days, stocks with new 6-month highs or lows, stocks with a low above yesterday's high or a high below yesterday's low, and stocks which have traded twice their average volume. See Appendix F for a list of optionable stocks.

Updated daily. **$**

12.8.4
Commodity Markets **COMMODITIES**

CompuServe offers access to historical information on commodities futures and cash prices along with exclusive newsletters offering news, features, recommendations and analysis.

CompuServe's commodities database contains open, high, low, settling, and cash prices along with volume and open interest for every trading day since January, 1979. Futures prices are generally available by 6:00 p.m. Eastern time with the cash price, volume, and open interest available 24 hours later. The data is provided by MJK Associates which uses multiple sources to ensure accuracy and guarantee timeliness. Data is available for all commodities on the U.S. or Canadian exchanges with significant trading volume. Data includes financial and currency futures as well as metal, petroleum, and agricultural commodity contracts. Composite prices from Commodity Research Bureau are also available. A list of Commodity Symbols can be found in Appendix I.

12.8.4.1
Commodity Pricing — One Contract, Many Days **CPRICE**

Pricing History — One Contract presents historical performance by day, week, or month for the requested delivery period for the requested commodity (or optionally the nearest delivery). The program displays open, high, low and settling prices along with volume and open interest. Also available are aggregated volume and open interest for all contracts for the requested commodity along with the cash market price for the commodity. A list of commodity symbols can be found in Appendix I.

Updated daily. **$**

12

12.8.4.2
News-a-tron Market Reports **NAT**
Refer to 12.5.4

12.8.4.3
Agri-Commodities, Inc. **ACI**
Futures Focus is a weekly newsletter for the futures trader published by Agri-Commodities, a leading agricultural and futures consultant to governments and corporations worldwide. It features the TSF trading system, trading recommendations, a market overview and tips on how to improve one's trading performance. Updated weekly. See Appendix E for a list of popular market indicators. **$**

12.8.5
No-Load Mutual Funds **NOLOAD**
The No-Load Mutual Fund Association provides extensive information regarding no-load and low-load mutual funds currently available on the market including a one paragraph overview of the fund's objective and its strategy for achieving that objective. Fund information may be retrieved by designating the fund manager, the fund name, the strategy of the fund, the initial investment requirement, and several other criteria. Each fund displays the above information as well as the CompuServe and the NASD ticker symbol, and key features for the fund. Requests for additional information on specific funds can be entered online and will be forwarded to the funds for mail reply. See Appendix D for a list of popular mutual fund symbols.
     Updated monthly.

12.8.6
Investment Analysis **ANALYSIS**
Investment Analysis menu selections offer various methods of using MicroQuote II investment data. Disclosure Screening and Securities Screening give subscribers the opportunity to search the entire Disclosure universe of our 9,000 companies or the MicroQuote universe of our 90,000 securities respectively for prospective purchase candidates. Return Analysis and Portfolio Valuation can then be used to track purchased securities and gauge your success.

12

12.8.6.1
Company Screening   **COSCREEN**
Company Screening makes it possible to screen the Disclosure II database based on
entered criteria and produce a list of companies that meet the criteria. The ticker symbols
of the companies can be saved for use in other CompuServe programs. Selection criteria
include a variety of growth rates and financial ratios along with SIC codes, state, total
assets, book value, market value, annual sales, net income, cash flow, latest price, etc.
See Appendix F for a list of optionable stocks.
    Updated weekly with market prices updated daily. **$E**

12.8.6.2
Securities Screening   **SCREEN**
This product enables you to enter selected investment criteria and then screen the
MicroQuote II database to see what securities meet your criteria. You can search on latest
price, exchange, beta, earnings, SIC code or similar criteria. Selection criteria include a
variety of growth rates and financial ratios along with SIC codes, state, total assets, book
value, market value, annual sales, net income, cash flow, latest stock prices, etc. See
Appendixes D, E and F for lists of symbols used in this product.
    Securities Screening is useful for buying into or selling short and for picking bonds
with specific maturity dates and yield targets. It is updated weekly with market prices
updated daily. **$E**

12.8.6.3
Return Analysis   **RETURN**
Return Analysis calculates the holding period and annualized returns for as many as 30
requested securities. Symbols specifying the issues may be entered at the terminal or
from a stored file. Since the subscriber enters the holding period, this product is useful for
analyzing the historical performances of specific issues such as mutual funds in bull and
bear markets. See Appendixes D, E, F, G and H for lists of symbols used in this product.
    Updated daily. **$E**

12.8.6.4
Portfolio Valuation   **PORT**
Portfolio Valuation finds the value of a previously created portfolio for dates you select
and displays unrealized gains and losses. See Appendixes D, E, F, G and H for lists of
symbols used in this product.
    Updated daily. **$**

12.8.7
Issue/Symbol Lookup   **SYMBOLS**

Through this menu you can determine what securities and indexes are included in MicroQuote II and the access symbol for each. Updated daily.

12.8.7.1
Search For Company Name, Ticker Symbol or CUSIP   CUSIP

This program will search by name, CUSIP number, or ticker symbol and list all the issues for a company you select. The program displays the ticker symbol, CUSIP number, exchange code and the name and description for each issue. See Appendixes D, E, F, G and H for lists of symbols used in this product. **$**

12.8.7.2
List Bonds For Company   **BONDS**

Bonds Listing displays all active bonds for the designated company. The report includes the ticker symbols, the CUSIP numbers, an issue description, and the yield and the current selling price for each bond. Also included in the report is the quality rating expressed by both Standard & Poor's and Moody's. See Appendix F for a list of optionable stocks.
    Updated daily. **$**

12.8.7.3
Menu of Available Indexes   **INDICATORS**

This product gives the ticker and the CUSIP number for all indexes included in the MicroQuote II database along with the time period for which each index has data. Issues are categorized in manageable groups designated by Market/Industry Indexes, Bonds/Yields, Exchange Rates, Volumes, Advances and Declines, and any issues which are new or do not fall into one of the previous categories. An option is available which lists all indexes without going through the menus. Each index is updated daily. Lists of Market Indicators, Bond Yield Indicators and Exchange Rate Symbols can be found in Appendixes E, G and H respectively.

12.8.7.4
Menu of Available Commodities   **CSYMBOL**

Commodity Group Listing displays available commodity groups including foods, woods, grains/feeds, fats/oils, metals, financial, petroleum, fibers, currencies and indexes. Access symbols, exchange, and issue description are shown for each commodity. A list of Commodity Symbols can be found in Appendix I.

12

12.9
Other Interests   **OTHER**

This is a miscellaneous category.

12.9.1
Military Veterans Services   **VET**

The Military Vets Forum encourages discussion of current topics, and includes a personal adjustment section for Vets to inquire about problems, data library files on veterans benefits, the MIA/POW issue, Agent Orange, Atomic Vets, Veterans Organizations and member writings. The complete list of the names on the Vietnam Veterans Memorial and a direct connection to CDC on the Agent Orange Studies is included. A CompuServe Forum and Buddy Locator are available to veterans only.

12.9.2
Rapaport's Diamond Service   **RDC**

Rapaport Diamond Corporation provides information about diamonds and the diamond trade and enables professionals to buy and sell diamonds. It gives background and general information about diamonds, detailed price information on diamond trading, a trading section that lists stones currently for sale as well as buy requests, diamond market reports, special diamond reports, letters to the system and auction reviews. Registered traders can update the database and have access to additional diamond data.

12

12.9.3
Real Estate   **REAL ESTATE**

World-Wide Investment System enables you to predict an investment's outcome. It allows you to calculate investments and appraisals based on your investment expectations. You can also receive an appraised price. WIS is a safeguard for your investments. It tells you what price to pay before investing or what return to expect after investing.

12.9.4
Professional Forums   **PROFORUM**

This section contains forums for lawyers, doctors and other professionals and those interested in professional fields.

12.9.4.1
PR and Marketing Forum   **PRSIG**
Refer to 12.2.2

12.9.4.2
Legal Forum   **LAWSIG**
Refer to 12.7.1

12.9.4.3
AAMSI Medical Forum   **MEDSIG**
Refer to 12.6.1

12.9.4.4
Safetynet   **SAFETYNET**
Refer to 12.5.3

12.9.4.5
Autodesk Forum   **ADESK**
Refer to 12.5.1

12.9.4.7
Computer Training Forum   **DPTRAIN**
Refer to 12.2.8

12

12.9.4.8
Military Veterans Forum   **VETSIG**
This forum enables veterans to gain and exchange information. It includes information on veterans benefits, Vietnam veterans information and a buddy locator service.

12.9.4.10
Computer Consultant's Forum   **CONSULT**
Refer to 12.3.3

12.9.4.11
Health Forum   **GOODHEALTH**
Health Forum provide the subscriber with general health-related information. Included are discussions on fitness and emotional and family health. Every Friday night a "Trivia Night" is held where the professional or non-professional may answer health-related questions.

12.9.4.12
Int'l Entrepreneurs Network   **USEN**
Refer to 12.2.3

12.9.5
FBI Ten Most Wanted   **FBI**
The FBI's current Ten Most Wanted Fugitives are listed including biographical information, crimes and pictures. It also gives information on FBI past fugitives including stories of their apprehensions. To obtain the fugitives' pictures, your terminal must support the graphics mode.

12.9.6
IQuest   **IQU**
Refer to 12.2.6

12.9.7
Information USA   **INFOUSA**
Refer to 12.2.7

12.9.7.12
Electronic Answer Man   **EAM**
Refer to 12.2.7.12

12

APPENDIXES

A

There are three ways to navigate on the CompuServe System: Menu Choices, GO Commands and Other Commands.

Menu Choices are the easiest to use and understand. You can branch down from the top menu through submenus to each product on the CompuServe Information Service. The organization of the Almanac reflects the menu structure as it existed when the Almanac was written. So if the description of the product you want to use is located in Chapter 3, enter menu choice 3, COMMUNICATIONS/BULLETIN BOARDS. Then choose the section that you think should contain the product. Remember that product descriptions close to the beginning of a chapter will be close to the top of the menu and conversely. A variation of menu choices is the product number described previously.

GO Commands can be used with a Quick Reference Word or a Page Number to "jump" from one product to another without branching through menus. We have included the Quick Reference Word or page number for the products in the Almanac. Page numbers change frequently so we have provided room in the Almanac for you to write them down. Also page numbers can get you to exactly where you want to go in a product, so you will want to write down the page numbers of your most frequently used areas. The page number or Quick Reference Word appears in the upper right-hand corner of most screens.

Other Commands such as the Top command can be found in your Users Guide. The most commonly used ones are included for your reference in the Brief Command Summary at the end of this section.

Some products are placed on more than one menu. Occasionally you may find that you exit a product into a different menu than the one you used to enter it. We encourage you to explore the new menu of related products. If you wish to return to the original menu, you can use the GO command, or you can return to the top menu and branch down.

Brief Command Summary

The most commonly used commands are listed here for your convenience. For a complete list, consult your Users Guide.

Every command must end with a carriage return. Pressing the carriage return key (which may be marked ENTER on some keyboards) transmits the command to CompuServe. In online information, the carriage return key is represented by the symbol ⟨CR⟩ or the word ENTER.

T — TOP	Goes directly to the first page (TOP) of CompuServe. This is sometimes called the TOP menu.
M — Menu	Goes back to the menu that points to the current page. A single ⟨CR⟩ will also return to the last menu if there isn't a next page.
H or ? — HELP	Displays a list of commands which are available to use at that prompt.
S n — SCROLL n	SCROLLs information display continuously without pausing. At a menu prompt, S n displays item n by scrolling through all pages for that item. (Please note that a space is required between the S and item n.)

B — BACKWARD   Displays the page preceding the current page.

R — RESEND   Redisplays the current page. This is useful if the current page has scrolled off the screen or after a HELP command.

FIND topic   Finds all index references to a topic and displays a menuized list with corresponding Quick Reference Words or page numbers. "topic" is the keyword you enter.

N — NEXT   Selects the NEXT item from last menu and displays it. For example, if 5 was the last choice, N will display item 6.

P — PREVIOUS   Selects the PREVIOUS item from last menu. For example, if 5 was the last choice, P will display item 4.

F — FORWARD   Displays the next page in a series of pages. A single ⟨CR⟩ will do the same thing.

Control Character Commands

Control characters transmit special commands to the host computer. These commands are entered by pressing two keys simultaneously: the Control key and a letter key. Pressing the control key by itself does not cause any action. The control key can be held down before, during, and after pressing the letter key.

| Control C | Stops the current action. You then can type another menu selection or command. ^C is displayed on your screen. |

Control O   Discontinues the display of information. ^O is displayed on your screen.

Control A   Suspends output from the host computer at the end of the line.

Control Q or Control W   Resumes the display after a Control A.

Control U   When entered in a line you are typing, the line currently being typed is deleted. ^U is displayed.

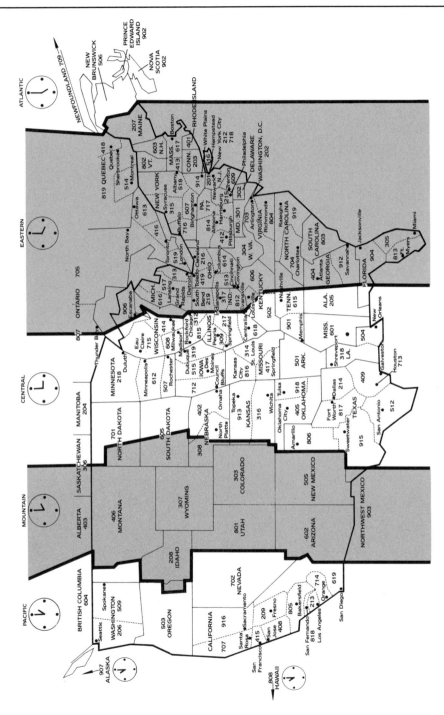

APPENDIX C: *State and Province Codes*

These codes are used in many products and are especially useful in searching databases. Weather and travel products use these codes.

State or Province	Code	State or Province	Code
Alabama	AL	New Brunswick	NB
Alaska	AK	New Hampshire	NH
Alberta	AB	New Jersey	NJ
Arizona	AZ	New Mexico	NM
Arkansas	AR	New York	NY
British Columbia	BC	Newfoundland	NF
California	CA	North Carolina	NC
Colorado	CO	North Dakota	ND
Connecticut	CT	Nova Scotia	NS
Delaware	DE	Northwest Territories	NT
Dist Of Columbia	DC	Ohio	OH
Florida	FL	Oklahoma	OK
Georgia	GA	Ontario	ON
Idaho	ID	Oregon	OR
Illinois	IL	Pennsylvania	PA
Indiana	IN	Prince Edward Island	PE
Iowa	IA	Quebec	PQ
Kansas	KS	Rhode Island	RI
Kentucky	KY	Saskatchewan	SK
Louisiana	LA	South Carolina	SC
Maine	ME	South Dakota	SD
Manitoba	MB	Tennessee	TN
Maryland	MD	Texas	TX
Massachusetts	MA	Utah	UT
Michigan	MI	Vermont	VT
Minnesota	MN	Virginia	VA
Mississippi	MS	Washington	WA
Missouri	MO	West Virginia	WV
Montana	MT	Wisconsin	WI
Nebraska	NE	Wyoming	WY
Nevada	NV	Yukon	YK

APPENDIX D: *Popular Mutual Funds*

The following list of popular mutual funds was extracted from the MicroQuote II database. To find the symbols for other mutual funds, use the Ticker and Cusip Lookup Program (GO CUSIP).

Mutual Fund Name	Ticker	Mutual Fund Name	Ticker
Acorn Fd Inc	ACRNX	Dean Witter Tx Adv Corp Tr Sh Ben Int	DWTAX
Afuture Fd Inc	AFUTX	Dean Witter u s Govt Secs Tr Sh Ben Int	DWUSX
Amev Cap Fd Inc	AMCLX	Dean Witter World Wide Invt Sh Ben Int	DWWWX
Amev Money Fd Inc	AVMXX	Depositors Fd Boston Inc	DEPTX
Amev Spl Fd Inc	AMSLX	Double Exempt Flex Fd Inc	DEFFX
Amev U S Govt Secs Fd Inc	AMUGX	Dreyfus a Bds Plus Inc	DRBDX
Babson D I Bond Trust Sh Ben Int	BABIX	Dreyfus Calif Tax Ex Bd Fd	DRCAX
Babson D I Money Mkt Fd Inc Prime Portfolio	BMMXX	Dreyfus Fd Inc	DREVX
Babson D I Tax Free Income F Com Portfolio I	BALTX	Dreyfus Gnma Fd Inc	DRGMX
Babson David I Growth Fd Inc	BABSX	Dreyfus Growth Oppt Fd Inc	DREQX
Babson Enterprise Fd Inc	BABEX	Dreyfus Insd Tax Exmpt Bd Fd	DTBDX
Babson Value Fd Inc	BVALX	Dreyfus Instl Mkt Fd Inc Com Govt Secs	DINXX
Beacon Hill Mut Fd Inc	BEHMX	Dreyfus Instl Mkt Fd Inc Com Money Mkt	DMSXX
Benham Calif Tax Free Tr Inter Trm Portf	BCITX	Dreyfus Inter Tax Ex Bd Fd	DITEX
Benham Calif Tax Free Tr Long Trm Portf	BCLTX	Dreyfus Leverage Fd Inc	DRLEX
Benham Natl Tax Free Tr Mny Mkt Portfol	BNTXX	Dreyfus Liquid Assets Inc	DLAXX
Boston Co Fd Fd Sh Ben Int	BCCAX	Dreyfus Mass Tx Exempt Bd Fd Sh Ben Int	DMEBX
Boston Co Fd Managd Inc Fd	BOSGX	Dreyfus Money Mkt Instrs Inc Com-govt Secs	DMMXX
Boston Co Fd Sh Ben Int	BCAXX	Dreyfus Money Mkt Instrs Inc Com-money Mkt	DMIXX
Boston Co Fd Spl Gwth Fd Sbi	BOSSX	Dreyfus N Y Tax Ex Bd Fd Inc	DRNYX
Boston Co Tax Free Mun Fds Mass Tx Free Ny	BCMXX	Dreyfus New Leaders Fd Inc	DNLDX
Bull & Bear Cap Grwth Fd Inc	BULSX	Dreyfus Spl Income Fd Inc	DRSPX
Bull & Bear Equity Inc Fd	BULAX	Dreyfus Tax Exempt Bd Fd Inc	DRTAX
Bull & Bear Hi Yield Fd Inc	BULHX	Dreyfus Tax Exempt Money Mkt	DTEXX
Bull & Bear Inc Dlr Resvs Stk	BULXX	Dreyfus Third Centy Fd Inc	DRTHX
Bullock Agressive Gwth Shs	CABAX	Evergreen Fd Inc	EVGRX
Bullock Balanced Shs Inc	CABNX	Evergreen Total Return Fd	EVTRX
Bullock Dividends Shs Inc	CABDX	Exchange Fd Boston Inc	EXCHX
Bullock Fd Ltd	CABBX	Explorer Fd Inc	VEXPX
Bullock High Income Shs Inc	CABHX	Explorer Ii Fd Inc	VEIIX
Bullock Tax Free Shs Inc	CABTX	Fidelity Calif Tax Free Fd High Yld	FCTFX
Bullock U S Govt Inc Shs Inc	CBGIX	Fidelity Calif Tax Free Fd Shrt Term Port	FCFXX
Calvert Cash Resvs Prime Portfolio	CPRXX	Fidelity Cash Resvs Sh Ben Int	FDRXX
Calvert Cash Resvs U S Treas Potfl	CTUXX	Fidelity Congress Str Fd Inc	CNGRX
Calvert Fd Equity Portfolio	CFEQX	Fidelity Contrafund Inc	FCNTX
Calvert Fd Wash Area Gwth	WGRFX	Fidelity Corporate Tr Adj Rt Pfd Port	FCPTX
Calvert Rd Incom Portfolio	CFICX	Fidelity Daily Income Tr Sh Ben Int	FDTXX
Calvert Social Invt Fd Mngd Growth Ptf	CSIFX	Fidelity Discoverer Fd Sh Ben Int	FDLAX
Calvert Social Invt Fd Money Mkt Prtfl	CSIXX	Fidelity Equity-income Fd In	FEQIX
Calvert Tax Free Resvs Long Term Port	CTTLX	Fidelity Exchange Fd Shs	FDLEX
Calvert Tax Free Resvs Ltd Term Portfo	CTFLX	Fidelity Fd Inc	FFIDX
Calvert Tax Free Resvs Mm Portfolio	CTMXX	Fidelity Flexible Bd Fd	FBNDX
Charter Fd Inc	CHTRX	Fidelity Freedom Fd Sh Ben Int	FDFFX
De Vegh Mut Fd Inc	DEVGX	Fidelity Govt Secs Fd Ltd Ltd Partnership	FGOVX
Dean Witter Conv Secs Tr Sh Ben Int	DWSCX	Fidelity High Income Fd	FAGIX
Dean Witter Developing Gwth Sh Ben Int	DWDGX	Fidelity High Yield Muns	FHIGX
Dean Witter Dividend Growth	DWDVX	Fidelity Income Fd Mtg Secs Port	FMSFX
Dean Witter Hi Yield	DWHYX	Fidelity Ltd Term Muns Sh Ben Int	FLTMX
Dean Witter Indexed Valued	DWIVX	Fidelity Magellan Fd Inc	FMAGX
Dean Witter N Y Tx Fr Income Sh Ben Int	DWNYX	Fidelity Mass Tax Free Fd Money Mkt Portf	FDMXX
Dean Witter Natl Res Dev	DWNAX	Fidelity Mass Tax Free Fd Muni Bd Portfol	FDMMX
Dean Witter Opt Inc Tr Sh Ben Int	DWOPX	Fidelity Mercury Fd Sh Ben Int	FDMFX
Dean Witter Sears Liquid	DWLXX	Fidelity Money Mkt Tr Sh Mon Mkt	FMDXX
Dean Witter Sears U S Gvt Tr Sh Ben Int	DWGXX	Fidelity Money Mkt Tr Sh Us Govt Prtf	FMGXX
Dean Witter Tax Exempt	DWTEX	Fidelity Money Mkt Tr Sh Us Treas Pr	FTPXX
Dean Witter Tax Free Income Sh Ben Int	DWCTX	Fidelity Mun Bd Fd Inc	FMBDX

Mutual Fund Name	Ticker	Mutual Fund Name	Ticker
Fidelity N Y Tax Free Fd Muni Bd Portflo	FTFMX	Franklyn N Y Tax Free Income	FNYTX
Fidelity Overseas Fd Sh Ben Int	FOSFX	Gateway Opt Income Fd Inc	GATEX
Fidelity Puritan Fd Inc	FPURX	Good & Bad Times Fd Inc	GBTFX
Fidelity Qualified Divi Fd	FQDFX	Hartwell Growth Fd Inc	HRGRX
Fidelity Secs Fd Otc Portfolio	FOCPX	Hartwell Leverage Fd Inc	HRTLX
Fidelity Select Portfolios Leisure & Entm	FDLSX	Hutton Ama Cash Fd Inc	HCSXX
Fidelity Select Portfolios Brkge & Invt Pt	FSLBX	Hutton Calif Mun Fd Inc	HCMUX
Fidelity Select Portfolios Chems Portfolio	FSCHX	Hutton Govt Fd Inc	HGFXX
Fidelity Select Portfolios Computers Port	FDCPX	Hutton Invt Ser Inc Basic Value Ser	EFBVX
Fidelity Select Portfolios Defense & Aeros	FSDAX	Hutton Invt Ser Inc Emerging Gwth	HERGX
Fidelity Select Portfolios Electrs Port	FSELX	Hutton Invt Ser Inc Govt Secs Ser	HGVSX
Fidelity Select Portfolios Energy Port	FSENX	Hutton Invt Ser Inc Opt Income Ser	OPTNX
Fidelity Select Portfolios Finl Svcs Prtfl	FIDSX	Hutton Invt Ser Inc Precious Metals	EFPMX
Fidelity Select Portfolios Food & Agric Pt	FDFAX	Hutton Invt Ser Ins Bond Trm Invt	HBDIX
Fidelity Select Portfolios Health Care Ptf	FSPHX	Hutton Invt Ser Ins Gwth Trm Invt	HGRWX
Fidelity Select Portfolios Prec Metal Min	FDPMX	Hutton N Y Mun Fd Inc	HNYMX
Fidelity Select Portfolios Sftwre & Comp	FSCSX	Hutton Natl Mun Fd Inc	HNAMX
Fidelity Select Portfolios Svgs & Ln Port	FSVLX	I D S New Dimensions Fd Inc	INNDX
Fidelity Select Portfolios Tech Portfolio	FSPTX	I D S Progressive Fd Inc	INPRX
Fidelity Select Portfolios Telecomm Port	FSTCX	Ids Bd Fd Inc	INBNX
Fidelity Select Portfolios Utility Port	FSUTX	Ids Cash Mgmt Fd Inc	IDSXX
Fidelity Spl Situations Fd Sh Ben Int	FSLSX	Ids Discovery Fd Inc	INDYX
Fidelity Tax Exempt Money Mk Sh Ben Int	FTEXX	Ids Extra Income Fd Inc	INEAX
Fidelity Thrift Tr Sh Ben Int	FTHRX	Ids Growth Fd Inc	INIDX
Fidelity Trend Fd Inc	FTRNX	Ids High Yield Tax Exempt Fd	INHYX
Fidelity U S Govt Resvs	FGRXX	Ids Precious Metals Fd Inc	INPMX
Financial Bd Shs Inc Hi Yld Bd Port	FHYPX	Ids Selective Fund Inc	INSEX
Financial Bd Shs Inc Select Incom Pf	FBDSX	Ids Stock Fund	INSTX
Financial Daily Income Shs i	FDSXX	Ids Strategy Fd Inc Aggres Eq Port	INAGX
Financial Dynamics Fd Inc	FIDYX	Ids Strategy Fd Inc Equity Portfol	INEGX
Financial Indl Fd Inc	FLRFX	Ids Strategy Fd Inc Income Portfoli	ININX
Financial Indl Income Fd	FIIIX	Ids Strategy Fd Inc Money Mkt Portf	ISTXX
Financial Planners Fed Secs Sh Ben Int	SFDXX	Ids Tax Free Money Fd Inc	ITFXX
Financial Tax Free Income Sh	FTIFX	Income Boston Fd	EVIBX
Finl Progressive World Tech	FPWTX	Investment Tr Boston Ctf Ben Int	IVTBX
First Variable Rate Fd For	FVRXX	Istel Fd Inc	ISTLX
Flex Fd Sh Ben Int	FLFDX	Ivy Growth Fund	IVYFX
Flex Fund Money Mkt Fd	FFMXX	Janus Fd Inc	JANSX
44 Wall Str Equity Fd Inc	FWLEX	Janus Value Fd Inc	JAVLX
44 Wall Str Fd Inc	FWALX	Janus Venture Fd Inc	JAVTX
Founders Growth Fd Inc	FRGRX	Kemper Calif Tax Free Incom	KCTFX
Founders Income Fd Inc	FRINX	Kemper Govt Money Mkt Fd Inc	KEGXX
Founders Money Mkt Fd Inc	FMMXX	Kemper Growth Fd Inc	KPGRX
Founders Mut Fd Shs Ben Int	FRMUX	Kemper High Yield Fd Inc	KMHYX
Founders Spl Fd Inc	FRSPX	Kemper Income & Cap	KMICX
Franklin Calif Tax Free Inc	FKTFX	Kemper Intl Fd Inc	KMIFX
Franklin Calif Tx Free Tr Tx Exmpt Mon Fd	FCLXX	Kemper Money Mkt Fd Inc	KMMXX
Franklin Corp Cash Mgmt Fd	FCCMX	Kemper Mun Bd Fd Inc	KPMBX
Franklin Custodian Fds Inc Dynatech Ser	FKDNX	Kemper Opt Income Fd Inc	KMOPX
Franklin Custodian Fds Inc Growth Ser	FKGRX	Kemper Summit Fd Inc	KMSMX
Franklin Custodian Fds Inc Income Ser	FKINX	Kemper Total Return Fd Inc	KMRTX
Franklin Custodian Fds Inc U S Govt Ser	FKUSX	Kemper U S Govt Secs Fd Inc Sh Ben Int	KPGVX
Franklin Custodian Fds Inc Util Ser	FKUTX	Lehman Cap Fd Inc	LMCPX
Franklin Equity Fd	FKREX	Lehman Invs Fd Inc	LINFX
Franklin Fedl Tax Free Incom	FKTIX	Lehman Mgmt Mm Fds Inc Cash Resvs Fd	LCRXX
Franklin Gold Fd	FKRCX	Lehman Mgnt Gvt Fds Inc Govt Resvs Fd	LGRXX
Franklin Money Fd	FMFXX	Lehman Opportunity Fund	LOPPX
Franklin Money Fd Ii	FMNXX	Leverage Fd Boston Inc	LEVGX
Franklin Opt Fd Inc	FKBRX	Lexington Gnma Income Fd Inc	LEXNX
Franklin Tax Exempt Money Fd	FTMXX	Lexington Goldfund Inc	LEXMX
Franklin Tax Free Tr Mich Insd	FTTMX	Lexington Govt Secs Mny Mkt	LSGXX
Franklin Tax Free Tr Mnn Insd Inc Fd	FMINX	Lexington Growth Fd Inc	LEXGX

APPENDIX D: *Popular Mutual Funds*

Mutual Fund Name	Ticker	Mutual Fund Name	Ticker
Lexington Money Mkt Tr Sh Ben Int	LMMXX	Provident Fd Income Inc	AGPRX
Lexington Resh Fd Inc	LEXRX	Putnam George Fd Boston Shs Ben Int	PGEOX
Lexington Tax Free Daily	LTFXX	Quest For Value Fd Inc	QFVFX
Lindner Divid Fd Inc	LDDVX	Rainbow Fd Inc	RBOWX
Lindner Fd Inc	LDNRX	Rowe Price Intl Fd Inc	PRITX
Lmh Fd Ltd	LMHFX	Rowe Price New Era Fd Inc	PRNEX
Loomis Sayles Cap Dev Fd Inc	LOMCX	Rowe Price New Horizons Fd i	PRNHX
Loomis Sayles Mut Fd Inc	LOMMX	Rowe Price New Income Fd Inc	PRCIX
Manhattvs Fd	CNAMX	Rowe Price Prime Resv Fd Inc	PRRXX
Merrill Lynch Basic Value Fd	MLBVX	Rowe Price Tax Free Income f	PRTAX
Merrill Lynch Cap Fd Inc	MLCPX	Rowe T Price Equity Inc Fd	PRFDX
Merrill Lynch Corp Bd Fd Inc High Income Pot	MLHIX	Rowe T Price GNMA Fd Sh Ben Int	PRGMX
Merrill Lynch Corp Bd Fd Inc High Qual Portf	MLHQX	Rowe T Price Growth & Income	PRGIX
Merrill Lynch Corp Bd Fd Inc Inter Term Potf	MLITX	Rowe T Price New Amer Grwth Sh Ben Int	PRWAX
Merrill Lynch Corp Divid Fd	MLQDX	Rowe T Price Tax Exempt Mone	PTEXX
Merrill Lynch Equi Bd i Fd i	MLEBX	Rowe T Price Tax Free Sht	PRFSX
Merrill Lynch Fd For Tomorro	MLFTX	Rowe T Price U S Treas Money	PRTXX
Merrill Lynch Govt Fd Inc	MLGXX	Royce Value Fund Inc	RYVFX
Merrill Lynch Instl Fd Inc	MLIXX	Safeco Equity Fd Inc	SAFQX
Merrill Lynch Instl Tx Ex Fd Sh Ben Int	MLEXX	Safeco Growth Fd Inc	SAFGX
Merrill Lynch Intl Hldgs Inc	MLHDX	Safeco Income Fd Inc	SAFIX
Merrill Lynch Mun Bd Fd Inc Com Hi Yld	MLHYX	Safeco Money Mkt Mut Fd Inc	SAFXX
Merrill Lynch Mun Bd Fd Inc Com Insd Portf	MLMBX	Safeco Mun Bd Fd Inc	SFCOX
Merrill Lynch Mun Bd Fd Inc Com Ltd Mat	MLLMX	Scudder Calif Tax Free Fd Sh Ben Int	SCTFX
Merrill Lynch Nat Res Tr Sh Ben Int	MLNRX	Scudder Cap Growth Fd Inc Cap Sh	SCDUX
Merrill Lynch Ny Mun Bd Fd Sh Ben Int	MLNYX	Scudder Cash Invt Tr Sh Ben Int	SCTXX
Merrill Lynch Pac Fd Inc	MLPAX	Scudder Dev Fd	SCDVX
Merrill Lynch Phoenix Fd Inc	MLPNX	Scudder Govt Money Fd	SCGXX
Merrill Lynch Ready Assets Sh Bn Int	MRAXX	Scudder Govt Mtg Secs Fd Sh Ben Int	SGMSX
Merrill Lynch Retirement Ben	MLYRX	Scudder Growth & Income Fd Sh Ben Int	SCDGX
Merrill Lynch Retirement Ser Sh Bn Int	MRRXX	Scudder Income Fd Inc	SCSBX
Merrill Lynch Spl Value Fd i	MLSVX	Scudder Intl Fd Inc	SCINX
Merrill Lynch U S A Gvt Resv Sh Ben Int	MGRXX	Scudder Managed Mun Bds Sh Ben Int	SCMBX
Mutual Beacon Fd	BEGRX	Scudder N Y Tax Free Fd Sh Ben Int	SCYTX
Mutual Shs Corp	MUTHX	Scudder Tax Free Money Fd Sh Ben Int	STFXX
Naess & Thomas Spl Fd Inc	NAESX	Scudder Tax Free Target Fd Sbi Prtfl 1990	STFTX
Neuwirth Fd Inc	NEUFX	Scudder Tax Free Target Fd Sbi Prtfl 1993	STTFX
Nicholas Fd Inc	NICSX	Scudder Tx Target Fd Sh Ben Int-port	STETX
Nicholas Ii Inc	NCTWX	Selected Amern Shs Inc	LISAX
Nicholas Income Fd Inc	NCINX	Selected Money Mkt Fd Inc	SMMXX
North Star Apollo Fd Inc	NSAFX	Selected Spl Shs Inc	LISSX
North Star Bd Fd Inc	NSBFX	Sequoia Fd Inc	SEQUX
North Star Regl Fd Inc	NSRFX	Shearson Aggresive Grwth Fd	SHRAX
North Star Stk Fd Inc	NSSFX	Shearson Appreciation Fd Inc	SHAPX
Paine Webber Amer Fd Inc	PWAMX	Shearson Cal Munis Inc	SHRCX
Paine Webber Atlas Fd Inc	PWATX	Shearson Daily Divid Inc	SDDXX
Paine Webber Cashfund Inc	PWCXX	Shearson Daily Tx Free Divid	SDTXX
Paine Webber Fixed Income GNMA Portfolio	PWGMX	Shearson Fundamental Val Fd	SHFVX
Paine Webber Fixed Income High Yld Port	PWHYX	Shearson Global Opports Fd Sh Ben Int	SHRGX
Paine Webber Fixed Income Invt Grd Bd Ptf	PIGPX	Shearson Govt & Agencies Inc	SHGXX
Paine Webber Tx Ex Incom Fd	PWTEX	Shearson High Yld Fd Inc	SHTRX
Painewebber Olympus Fd Inc	PWOFX	MUTUAL FUND NAME	TICKER
Pax World Fd Inc	PAXWX	Shearson Lehman Spl Port Lg Trm Gvt Inc	SHLGX
Penn Square Mut Fd Shs Ben Int	PESQX	Shearson Lehman Spl Ports Inter Term Gvt	SINGX
Pennsylvania Mut Fd Inc	PENNX	Shearson Lehman Spl Ports Opt Income Port	SOPTX
Pine Str Fd Inc	PINSX	Shearson Lehman Spl Potrs Tax Exmpt Incom	SXMTX
Plitrend Fd Inc	TRDFX	Shearson Managed Govts Inc	SHMGX
Price t Rowe Growth Stk Fd i	PRGFX	Shearson Managed Muns Inc	SHMMX
Price t Rowe High Yield Fd	PRHYX	Shearson N Y Muns Inc	SHNYX
Price t Rowe Tax Free High	PRFHX	State Bd Progress Fd Inc	STPRX
Pro Fd Inc	PRFNX	Stein Roe & Farnham Cap	SRFCX
Pro Income Fd Inc	PROIX	Stein Roe & Farnham Stk Fd i	SRFSX

237

Mutual Fund Name	Ticker	Mutual Fund Name	Ticker
Steinroe Cash Resvs Inc	STCXX	USAA Invt Tr Cornerstone Fd	USCRX
Steinroe Discovery Fd Inc	SRDFX	USAA Invt Tr Gold Fd	USAGX
Steinroe Govt Resvs Inc	SGRXX	USAA Money Market Fd Money Mkt Fd Sr	USAXX
Steinroe High Yield Muns Inc	SRMFX	USAA Mut Fd Inc Fed Secs MM Fd	OSFXX
Steinroe Inter Muns Inc	SRIMX	USAA Mutual Fd Inc Sunbelt Era Fd	USAUX
Steinroe Managed Bds Inc	SRBFX	USAA Tax Exempt Fd Inc High Yield Fd	USTEX
Steinroe Spl Fd Inc	SRSPX	USAA Tax Exempt Fd Inc Inter Term Fd	USATX
Steinroe Tax Ex Money Fd	STEXX	USAA Tax Exempt Fd Inc Short Term Fd	USSTX
Steinroe Tax Exempt Bd Fd In	SRFTX	Value Line Bd Fd Inc	VALBX
Steinroe Total Return Fd Inc	SRFBX	Value Line Cash Fd Inc	VLCXX
Steinroe Universe Fd Inc	SRUFX	Value Line Conv Fd Inc	VALCX
Stratton Growth Fd	STRGX	Value Line Fd Inc	VLIFX
Stratton Mnthly Divid Shs In	STMDX	Value Line Income Fd Inc	VALIX
Templeton Fds Inc World Fd	TEMWX	Value Line Leveraged Growth	VALLX
Twentieth Centy Invs Inc Giftrust Invs	TWGTX	Value Line Spl Situations Fd	VALSX
Twentieth Centy Invs Inc Growth Invs Shs	TWCGX	Value Line Tax Exempt Fd High Yld Port	VLHYX
Twentieth Centy Invs Inc Select Invs Sh	TWCIX	Value Line Tax Exempt Fd Inc Money Mkt Portf	VLTXX
Twentieth Centy Invs Inc U S Govt Sh	TWUSX	Vanguard Fixed Income Sec Fd GNMA Portfolio	VFIIX
Twentieth Centy Invs Inc Ultra Invs Sh	TWCUX	Vanguard Fixed Income Sec Fd High Yield Prtf	VWEHX
Twentieth Centy Invs Inc Vista Invs Sh	TWCVX	Vanguard Fixed Income Sec Fd Invt Grade Prtf	VWESX
Unified Growth Fd Inc	UNGFX	Vanguard Fixed Income Sec Fd Shtm Portfolio	VFSTX
Unified Income Fd Inc	UNIIX	Vanguard Index Tr Sh Ben Int	VFINX
Unified Mun Fd Inc Gen Ser	UNMGX	Vanguard Money Mkt Tr Fed Port	VMFXX
Unified Mun Fd Inc Ind Ser	UNMIX	Vanguard Money Mkt Tr Insd Portfolio	VMPXX
Unified Mut Shs Inc	UNFMX	Vanguard Money Mkt Tr Prime Port	VMMXX
United Cash Mgmt Inc	UNCXX	Vanguard Mun Bd Fd Inc High Yield Port	VWAHX
United Contl Growth Fd Inc	UNCGX	Vanguard Mun Bd Fd Inc Insd Lntrm Port	VILPX
United Contl Income Fd Inc	UNCIX	Vanguard Mun Bd Fd Inc Inter Term Port	VWITX
United Fds Inc Accum Fd Shs	UNACX	Vanguard Mun Bd Fd Inc Long Term Port	VWLTX
United Fds Inc Bond Fd Shs	UNBDX	Vanguard Mun Bd Fd Inc Mon Mkt Port	VMSXX
United Fds Inc Inc Fd Shs	UNCMX	Vanguard Mun Bd Fd Inc Shrt Term Port	VWSTX
United Fds Inc Science Fd Shs	UNSCX	Vanguard Qualified Divid Por	QDPTX
United Govt Secs Fd Inc Com New	UNGVX	Vanguard Specialized Portf Tech Portf	VGTCX
United High Income Fd Inc	UNHIX	Vanguard Specialized Portfl Gold & Prec Mtl	VGPMX
United Mun Bd Fd Inc	UNMBX	Vanguard Specialized Portfl Hlth Care Prtf	VGHCX
United New Concepts Fd Inc	UNEWX	Vanguard Specialized Portfl Svc Ecomy Ptfl	VGSEX
United Retirement Shs Inc	UNFDX	Vanguard Star Fd Sh Ben Int	VGSTX
United Svcs Fds Income Fd	USINX	Vanguard World Fd Intl Grwth Port	VWIGX
United Svcs Fds Lp Cap Fd	LOCFX	Vanguard World Fd U S Growth Port	VWUSX
United Svcs Fds New Prospect Fd	UNWPX	Wall Str Fd Inc	WALLX
United Svcs Gold Shs Inc	USERX	Wellesley Income Fd	VWINX
United Svcs Group Fds Inc Growth Fd	GRTHX	Wellington Fd Inc	VWELX
United Vanguard Fd Inc	UNVGX	Windsor Fd Inc	VWNDX
Uniteds Svcs Group Fds Inc Prospector Fd	PSPFX	Windsor Fd Inc Windsor Ii Prtf	VWNFX
USAA Growth Fund Growth Fd Ser	USAAX	World Trends Fd Sh Ben Int	WTFDX
USAA Income Fd Income Fd Ser	USAIX	Wpg Fund Inc	WPGFX

APPENDIX E: *Popular Market Indicators*

The following list of popular market indicators was extracted from the MicroQuote II database. To find the symbols for other market indicators, use the Ticker and Cusip Lookup Program (GO CUSIP).

Indicator Name	Ticker	Indicator Name	Ticker
Standard & Poors - 500 Composite	SP 500	Nasdaq - New Highs	XSUM H
Standard & Poors - 400 Industrials	SP 400	Nasdaq - New Lows	XSUM L
Standard & Poors - 20 Trans	SP 20	Nasdaq - Nasdaq 100 Indx	IXO
Standard & Poors - 40 Utilities	SP 40U	Wilshire 5000 - Index	WLSH
Standard & Poors - 40 Financial	SP 40F	Value Line - Industrial	VLII
Dow Jones - 30 Industrials	DJ 30	Value Line Comp Index - Index	XVL
Dow Jones - 65 Stk Composite	DJ 65	Moodys Util Stocks - 24 Util Com	MCBYU
Dow Jones - 20 Transports	DJ 20	New York Stock Exchange - Volume	NYSEL
Dow Jones - 15 Utilities	DJ 15	New York Stock Exchange - Up Volume	SP CJ
Dow Jones Commodity Index - Cmmdty Fut Idx	DJCI	New York Stock Exchange - Down Volume	SP CK
New York Stock Exchange - Industrials	NYII	American Stock Exchange - Volume	AMEXI
New York Stock Exchange - Transport	NYIT	American Stock Exchange - Up Volume	SP CL
New York Stock Exchange - Utilities	NYIU	American Stock Exchange - Down Volume	SP CM
New York Stock Exchange - Finance	NYIF	Nasdaq — Up Volume	XSUM U
NYSE Composite Index - Index	NYA	Nasdaq - Down Volume	XSUM D
Amex Composite Index	XAM1	Nasdaq - Unchanged Vol	XSUM N
Amex Major Mkt Index - Index	XMI	Nasdaq - Total Volume	XSUM V
Toronto - 300 Composite	CNXT	American Stock Exchange - Advances	AMEXF
Canadian Exchange Index - Montreal St Ex Index	CNXM	American Stock Exchange - Declines	AMEXJ
Nasdaq - Composite Index	COMP	American Stock Exchange - Unchanged	AMEXH
Nasdaq - Banking Stocks	BANK	New York Stock Exchange - Advances	NYSEI
Nasdaq - Industrials	INDS	New York Stock Exchange - Declines	NYSEJ
Nasdaq - Insurance Stks	INSR	New York Stock Exchange - Unchanged	NYSEK
Nasdaq - Financial Index	OFIN	Nasdaq — Advances	XSUM A
Nasdaq - Transportations	TRAN	Nasdaq — Declines	XSUM C
Nasdaq - Utilities Index	UTIL	Nasdaq — Unchanged	XSUM G

The following list was extracted from the MicroQuote II database and includes symbols for the most popular stocks. These are stocks which are so widely held that options on these stocks are also available. To find the symbols for other stocks use the Ticker and Cusip Lookup Program (GO CUSIP).

Company Name	Ticker	Company Name	Ticker
Aluminum Co Amer	AA	Baker Intl Corp	BKO
Alexander & Alexander Svcs	AAL	Bellsouth Corp	BLS
Abbott Labs	ABT	Bally Mfg Corp	BLY
Albany Intl Corp	ABY	Bristol Myers Co	BMY
American Can Co	AC	Borden Inc	BN
American Cyanamid Co	ACY	Burlington Northn Inc	BNI
Archer Daniels Midland Co	ADM	Bausch & Lomb Inc	BOL
American Elec Pwr Inc	AEP	Borg Warner Corp	BOR
Aetna Life & Cas Co	AET	Beatrice Cos Inc	BRY
American Gen Corp	AGC	Bethlehem Stl Corp	BS
Edwards A G Inc	AGE	Bear Sterns Cos Inc	BSC
Amerada Hess Corp	AHC	Bankers Tr N Y Corp	BT
Ahmanson H F & Co	AHM	Anheuser Busch Cos Inc	BUD
American Home Prods Corp	AHP	Chrysler Corp	C
American Hosp Supply Corp	AHS	Calfed Inc	CAL
American Intl Group Inc	AIG	Caterpillar Tractor Co	CAT
American Info Tech Corp	AIT	Caesars World Inc	CAW
Alcan Alum Ltd	AL	Cooper Inds Inc	CBE
Allied Corp	ALD	Chesebrough Ponds Inc	CBM
Arkla Inc	ALG	CBS Inc	CBS
Alaska Airls Inc	ALK	Commodore Intl Ltd	CBU
Allied Stores Corp	ALS	Capital Cities Communicatns	CCB
American Brands Inc	AMB	CCI Corp	CCI
Amdahl Corp	AMH	Control Data Corp Del	CDA
Advanced Micro Devices Inc	AMD	Comdisco	CDO
Amf Inc	AMF	Coastal Corp	CGP
American Med Intl Inc	AMI	Champion Intl Corp	CHA
Amp Inc	AMP	Carter Hawley Hale Stores	CHH
Amr Corp Del	AMR	Chemical New York Corp	CHL
Amax Inc	AMX	Churchs Fried Chicken Inc	CHU
Amoco Corp	AN	Chevron Corp	CHV
Apache Corp	APA	Cigna Corp	CI
Air Prods & Chems Inc	APD	Colgate Palmolive Co	CL
American President Cos Ltd	APS	Coleco Inds Inc	CLO
Asarco Inc	AR	Clorox Co Calif	CLX
Atlantic Richfield Co	ARC	Chase Manhattan Corp	CMB
Armco Inc	AS	Cmnty Psychiatric Ctrs Nev	CMY
ASA Ltd	ASA	Cincinnati Milacron Inc	CMZ
Ashland Oil Inc	ASH	Chicago & North Westn Transn	CNW
Automatic Data Processing	AUD	Colt Inds Inc	COT
Avon Prods Inc	AVP	Campbell Soup Co	CPB
Avnet Inc	AVT	Compaq Computer Corp	CPQ
American Express Co	AXP	Communications Satellite Co	CQ
Boeing Co	BA	Campbell Red Lake Mines Ltd	CRK
Bankamerica Corp	BAC	Computer Sciences Corp	CSC
Baxter Travenol Labs Inc	BAX	Combustion Engr Inc	CSP
Brunswick Corp	BC	CSX Corp	CSX
Boise Cascade Corp	BCC	Continental Telecom Inc	CTC
Bard C R Inc N J	BCR	Cullinet Software Inc	CUL
Becor Westn Inc	BCW	Computervision Corp	CVN
Black & Decker Corp	BDK	Commonwealth Edison Co	CWE
Becton Dickinson & Co	BDX	Cray Resh Inc	CYR
Bell Atlantic Corp	BEL	Celanese Corp	CZ
Beverly Enterprises	BEV	Dominion Res Inc Va	D
Browning Ferris Inds Inc	BFI	Delta Air Lines Inc	DAL
Burroughs Corp	BGH	Diebold Inc	DBD

APPENDIX F: *Optionable Stocks*

Company Name	Ticker	Company Name	Ticker
Du Pont E I De Nemours & Co	DD	General Instr Corp	GRL
Deere & Co	DE	Gillette Co	GS
Digital Equip Corp	DEC	Goodyear Tire & Rubr Co	GT
Dennys Inc	DEN	GTE Corp	GTE
Data Gen Corp	DGN	Gulf & Westn Inds Inc	GW
Dayton Hudson Corp	DH	Great Westn Finl Corp	GWF
Dresser Inds Inc	DI	Gencorp Inc	GY
Diamond Shamrock Corp	DIA	Halliburton Co	HAL
Disney Walt Prodtns	DIS	Hospital Corp Amer	HCA
Dart & Kraft Inc	DKI	Home Depot Inc	HD
Dome Mines Ltd	DM	Household Intl Inc	HI
Dun & Bradstreet Corp	DNB	Holiday Inns Inc	HIA
Dow Chem Co	DOW	Hitachi Ltd	HIT
National Distillers & Chem	DR	Hecla Mng Co	HL
Duke Pwr Co	DUK	Hilton Hotels Corp	HLT
Transco Energy Co	E	Homestake Mng Co	HM
Emery Air Fght Corp	EAF	Honda Mtr Ltd	HMC
Engelhard Corp	EC	Heinz H J Co	HNZ
Eckerd Jack Corp	ECK	Honeywell Inc	HON
Consolidated Edison Co N Y	ED	Hercules Inc	HPC
Hutton E F Group Inc	EFH	Harris Corp Del	HRS
Eastern Gas & Fuel Assoc	EFU	Hughes Tool Co	HT
EG & G Inc	EGG	Humana Inc	HUM
Eastman Kodak Co	EK	Hewlett Packard Co	HWP
Emerson Elec Co	EMR	International Business Machs	IBM
Ensearch Corp	ENS	IC Inds Inc	ICX
E Sys Inc	ESY	Intl Flavors & Fragrances	IFF
Coopervision Inc	EYE	Intl Minerals & Chem Corp	IGL
Ford Mtr Co Del	F	Internorth Inc	INI
First Boston Inc	FBC	International Paper Co	IP
Hall Frank B & Co Inc	FBH	Itt Corp	ITT
Federated Dept Stores Inc	FDS	Penney J C Inc	JCP
Federal Express Corp	FDX	Johnson & Johnson	JNJ
USF&G Corp	FG	Joy Mfg Co	JOY
Financial Corp Amer	FIN	Morgan J P & Co Inc	JPM
Firestone Tire & Rubr Co	FIR	Walter Jim Corp	JWC
Fleetwood Enterprises Inc	FLE	Kellogg Co	K
Fluor Corp Del	FLR	Kaneb Svcs Inc	KAB
First Chicago Corp	FNB	K Mart Corp	KM
Federal Natl Mtg Assn	FNM	Kerr Mcgee Corp	KMG
First Mississippi Corp	FRM	Coca Cola Co	KO
Freeport Mcmoran Inc	FTX	Lincoln Amern Corp N Y	LAC
Foster Wheeler Corp	FWC	Lehman Corp	LEM
Greyhound Corp	G	Litton Inds Inc	LIT
GAF Corp	GAF	Lockheed Corp	LK
GCA Corp	GCA	Louisiana Ld & Expl Co	LLX
Gannett Inc Del	GCI	Lilly Eli & Co	LLY
General Dynamics Corp	GD	Loral Corp	LOR
Golden West Finl Corp Del	GDW	Louisiana Pac Corp	LPX
General Elec Co	GE	Lear Siegler Inc	LSI
Genrad Inc	GEN	Limited Inc	LTD
General Mls Inc	GIS	Loews Corp	LTR
Gould Inc	GLD	LTV Corp	LTV
Corning Glass Wks	GLW	Southwest Airls Co	LUV
General Mtrs Corp	GM	M A Com Inc	MAI
General Mtrs Corp	GME	Mattel Inc	MAT
Golden Nugget Inc	GNG	MCA Inc	MCA
Georgia Pac Corp	GP	Mcdonalds Corp	MCD
Genuine Parts Co	GPC	Midcon Corp	MCN
Grumman Corp	GQ	Mcdonnell Douglas Corp	MD
Grace W R & Co	GRA	Mapco Inc	MDA
Gerber Scientific Inc	GRB	Mcdermott Intl Inc	MDR

Company Name	Ticker	Company Name	Ticker
Mohawk Data Sciences Corp	MDS	Phibro Salomon	PSB
Medtronic Inc	MDT	Pillsbury Co	PSY
Merrill Lynch & Co Inc	MER	Paine Webber Group Inc	PWJ
MGM Ua Entmt Co	MGM	Pennzoil Co	PZL
Manufacturers Hanover Corp	MHC	Rite Aid Corp	RAD
Mcgraw Hill Inc	MHP	Ralston Purina Co	RAL
Marriott Corp	MHS	Reading & Bates Corp	RB
Marion Labs Inc	MKC	Rca Corp	RCA
Mary Kay Cosmetics Inc	MKY	Royal Dutch Pete Co	RD
Martin Marietta Corp	ML	Rowan Cos Inc	RDC
Mesa Ltd Partnership	MLP	Ryder Sys Inc	RDR
Minnesota Mng & Mfg Co	MMM	Revco D S Inc	RDS
Philip Morris Inc	MO	Reynolds R J Inds Inc	RJR
Mobil Corp	MOB	Reynolds Metals Co	RLM
Motorola Inc	MOT	Rockwell Intl Corp	ROK
Merck & Co Inc	MRK	Rorer Group Inc	ROR
Mesa Pete Co	MSA	Raytheon Co	RTN
Middle South Utils Inc	MSU	Raychem Corp	RYC
Monsanto Co	MTC	Sears Roebuck & Co	S
Morton Thiokol Inc	MTI	Safeway Stores Inc	SA
Murphy Oil Corp	MUR	Sanders Assoc Inc	SAA
Macy R H & Co Inc	MZ	Sabine Corp	SAB
NBI Inc	NBI	Southwestern Bell Corp	SBC
Noble Affiliates Inc	NBL	Storer Communications Inc	SCI
NCR Corp	NCR	Scientific Atlanta Inc	SFA
NYSE Double Index	NDX	Santa Fe Southn Pac Corp	SFX
Newmont Mng Corp	NEM	Schering Plough Corp	SGP
NI Inds Inc	NL	Shaklee Corp	SHC
National Med Enterprises Inc	NME	Smith Intl Inc	SII
Northrop Corp	NOC	Smithkline Beckman Corp	SKB
Norfolk Southern Corp	NSC	Skyline Corp	SKY
National Semiconductor Corp	NSM	Schlumberger Ltd	SLB
Northern Telecom Ltd	NT	Southland Corp	SLC
Novo Industri A S	NVO	Sara Lee Corp	SLE
NWA Inc	NWA	Sea Ld Corp	SLN
NYSE Composite Index	NYA	Singer Co	SMF
NYNEX Corp	NYN	Sony Corp	SNE
Quaker Oats Co	OAT	Sonat Inc	SNT
Owens Corning Fiberglas Corp	OCF	Southern Co	SO
Ocean Drilling & Expl Co	ODR	Security Pac Corp	SPC
Owens Ill Inc	OI	Scott Paper Co	SPP
Occidental Pete Corp	OXY	Squibb Corp	SQB
Phillips Pete Co	P	Standard Oil Co	SRD
Pacific Telesis Group	PAC	Southland Rty Co	SRO
Pitney Bowes Inc	PBI	Sterling Drug Inc	STY
Penn Central Corp	PC	Sun Inc	SUN
Pittston Co	PCO	Sperry Corp	SY
Phelps Dodge Corp	PD	Sybron Corp	SYB
Paradyne Corp	PDN	Syntex Corp	SYN
Prime Mtr Inns Inc	PDQ	American Tel & Teleg Co	T
Panhandle Eastn Corp	PEL	Transamerica Corp	TA
Pepsico Inc	PEP	Tandy Corp	TAN
Pfizer Inc	PFE	Telex Corp	TC
Procter & Gamble Co	PG	Tidewater Inc	TDW
Pulte Home Corp	PHM	Teledyne Inc	TDY
Piedmont Aviation Inc	PIE	Tektronix Inc	TEK
Perkin Elmer Corp	PKN	Teradyne Inc	TER
Pioneer Corp Tex	PNA	Thrifty Corp	TFD
PPG Inds Inc	PPG	Tenneco Inc	TGT
Pogo Producing Co	PPP	Travelers Corp	TIC
Polaroid Corp	PRD	Time Inc	TL
Prime Computer Corp	PRM	Toys R Us	TOY

Company Name	Ticker	Company Name	Ticker
Trw Inc	TRW	Seagram Ltd	VO
Tesoro Pete Corp	TSO	Walgreen Co	WAG
Transworld Corp	TW	Warner Communications Inc	WCI
Texaco Inc	TX	Wendys Intl Inc	WEN
Texas Instrs Inc	TXN	Winnebago Inds Inc	WGO
Texas Oil & Gas Corp	TXO	Whittaker Corp	WKR
Textron Inc	TXT	Warner Lambert Co	WLA
Tri Contl Corp	TY	Williams Cos	WMB
U S Air Group Inc	U	Wal Mart Stores Inc	WMT
Ual Inc	UAL	Waste Mgmt Inc	WMX
Unocal Corp	UCL	Western Un Corp	WU
Union Carbide Corp	UK	Westinghouse Elec Corp	WX
Union Pac Corp	UNP	Weyerhaeuser Co	WY
Upjohn Co	UPJ	United States Stl Corp	X
U S West Inc	USW	Exxon Corp	XON
United Telecommunications	UT	Xerox Corp	XRX
United Technologies Corp	UTX	Woolworth F W Co	Z
Varian Assoc Inc	VAR	Crown Zellerbach Corp	ZB
Veeco Instrs Inc	VEE	Zenith Electrs Corp	ZE
Viacom Intl Inc	VIA	Zenith Labs Inc	ZEN
Valero Energy Corp	VLO	Zapata Corp	ZOS

APPENDIX G: *Exchange Rate Symbols*

The following list of exchange rate symbols was extracted from the MicroQuote II database. For a complete list, use The Menu of Available Indexes (GO INDICATORS).

Exchange Rate Name	Ticker
North/South America	
Canadian Dollar Xchg Rate - U S $ Per 100	CERT
Mexican Peso Xchg Rate - U S $ Per 10000	XRMP
European	
Austrian Schilling Xchg Rate - U S $ Per 100	XRAS
Belgian Franc Xchg Rate - U S $ Per 100	XRBF
British Pound Xchg Rate - U S $ Per 100	XRBP
Danish Krone Xchg Rate - U S $ Per 100	XRDK
Finnish Mark Exch Rate - Finland Mk Exch Rt	XFM
French Franc Xchg Rate - U S $ Per 100	XRFF
German Mark Xchg Rate - U S $ Per 100	XRGM
Greek Drachma Xchg Rate - U S $ Per 10000	XRGD
Irish Punt Exch Rate - Ireland Punt Exch Rt	XIP
Italian Lira Xchg Rate - U S $ Per 10000	XRIL
Luxembourg Franc Xchg Rate - U S $ Per 100	XRLF
Netherlands Guilder Xchg Rat - U S $ Per 100	XRNG

Exchange Rate Name	Ticker
European (continued)	
Norwegian Krone Xchg Rate - U S $ Per 100	XRNK
Portugese Escudo Xchg Rate - U S $ Per 10000	XRPE
Spanish Peseta Xchg Rate - U S $ Per 10000	XRSP
Swedish Krona Xchg Rate - U S $ Per 100	XRSK
Swiss Franc Xchg Rate - U S $ Per 100	XRSF
Asian	
Hong Kong Dollar Xchg Rate - U S $ Per 100	XRHD
Japanese Yen Xchg Rate - U S $ Per 10000	XRJY
Singapore Dollar Xchg Rate - U S $ Per 100	XRSD
Others	
Australian Dollar Xchg Rate - U S $ Per 100	XRAD
Israeli Shekel - U S $ Per 100	XRIS
Lebanese Pound Xchg Rate - U S $ Per 10000	XRIS
South African Rand Xchg Rate - U S $ Per 100	XRSR

APPENDIX H: *Popular Interest Rate Indicators*

The following list of popular interest rate indicators was extracted from the MicroQuote II database. For the complete list, use The Menu of Available Indexes (GO INDICATORS).

Indicator Name	Ticker	Indicator Name	Ticker
Certificate Of Deposit - 30-day Rate	CDRA	Lehman Brothers - Gvt/Corp Lg Trm	SONSB
Certificate Of Deposit - 60-day Rate	CDRB	Lehman Brothers - Govt Bonds	SONSE
Certificate Of Deposit - 90-day Rate	CDRC	Salomon Brothers Bond Index - High Grade	SALO
Commercial Paper - 30-day Rate	CPRA	Salomon Brothers Bond Index - a Rated	SP CO
Commercial Paper - 60-day Rate	CPRB	Salomon Brothers Bond Index — Composite	SP CEM
Commercial Paper - 90-day Rate	CPRC	Salomon Brothers Bond Index — Cum 1-2yr Govt	SALO06
U S Treasury Bill Yields - 91-day Bills	USTBA	Salomon Brothers Bond Index - Cum Mtg Overall	SALO14
U S Treasury Bill Yields - 182-day Bills	USTBB	Whites - Muni Bond Index	WHMI
U S Dollar Libor - 90-day Rate	LBRA	Standard & Poors - Municipal	MBI SP
U S Dollar Libor - 180-day Rate	LBRB	Municipal Bond Index - Bond Buyer 20 Bd Ave	MBI BB
U S Dollar Libor - 360-day Rate	LBRC	Bond Buyer Muni Bond Index - Futures Index	BBMB
Prime Interest Rate - U S Rate	PRMR	Bond Buyer - Muni Futures In	BBMI
Federal Funds - U S Rate	FFRT	Muni Bd Index Merrill 500 - Utility Rev	UNTO
Dow Jones Bond Averages - 10 Public Util	DJPU	Moodys Corp Bond Yields - AAA Corp Avg	MCBYA
Dow Jones Bond Averages - 10 Indust.	DJIL	Moodys Corp Bond Yields - AA Corp Avg	MCBYB
Dow Jones Averages - 20 Bonds	DJB	Moodys Corp Bond Yields - A Corp Avg	MCBYC
Municipal Bond Index - Dow Jones Muni Index	MBI DJ	Moodys Corp Bond Yields - Ind Yld Avg	MCBYF
Lehman Brothers - Corp Bond	SONSA	Moodys Corp Bond Yields - Util Yld Avg	MCBYK

APPENDIX I: *Commodity Symbols*

The following list of commodity symbols was complete when the Almanac was prepared. For the current list, use the Menu of Available Indexes program (GO CSYMBOL).

Chicago Board of Trade

#2 Yellow Chicago Soybeans	BEANS
Crude Petroleum Oil	CBTCP
Municipal Bond Index	CBTMB
Major Market Index	CBTMMI
Maxi Major Market Index	CBTXMMI
#2 Yellow Corn	CORN
30 Year 8% GNMAs	GNMA
Chicago 1 kg Gold	KGOLD
1,000 Ounce Chicago Silver	KSILVER
Soybean Meal	MEAL
#2 Heavy Chicago Oats	OATS
Crude Soybean Oil	OIL
15 Year U.S. T-Bonds	TBOND
10-year 8% Treasury Notes	TNOTE
#2 Red Chicago Wheat	WHEAT
Western Plywood	WPLYWOOD

Commodity Exchange, New York

Aluminum	ALUMINUM
100 Oz. New York Gold	COMGOLD
Copper	COPPER
Liquified Propane Gas	LPG
5,000 Oz. New York Silver	SILVER

Coffee, Sugar & Cocoa Exchange

Coffee C	COFFEE
Cocoa	MCOCOA
Sugar No. 11	SUGAR

New York Cotton Exchange

Cotton No. 2	COTTON
Frozen Concentrated Orange Juice	FCOJ

Chicago Mercantile Exchange

Feeder Steers	FDCATTLE
Pork Bellies	FZPK
Live Hogs	HOGS
Live Choice Steers	LCATTLE
Lumber	LUMBER

International Money Mart

British Pounds	BP
Canadian Dollars	CD
Deutsche Mark	DM
3 Month Domestic Cert. of Deposit	IMMDCD
3 Month Eurodollars	IMMEUD
100 Oz. IMM Gold	IMMGOLD
Japanese Yen	JY
Mexican Peso	PESO
Swiss Franc	SF
S&P 100 Stock Index	SP100
S&P 500 Stock Index	SP500
3 Month T-Bills	TBILL

Kansas City Board of Trade

Value Line Mini Index	KCMINIVL
Value Line Stock Index	KCVLI
#2 Hard Kansas City Wheat	KCWHEAT

Minneapolis Grain Exchange

#2 Northern Minnesota Spring Wheat	MNWHEAT

New York Futures Exchange

NYSE Composite Stock Index	NYSCI

New York Mercantile Exchange

Round White Cash Potatoes	CPOTS
Heating Oil #2	HO
Light Crude Oil	NYLCO
NY Harbor Leaded Regular Gas	NYLRG
Paladium	PALADIUM
Platinum	PLATINUM

Many guides and manuals are available to help you benefit from your CompuServe subscription. They range from service-specific users guides to game guides to cross-assembler guides. You can find a list and description of them by entering GO ORDER.

Price shown here are subject to change. Please check online for most current prices when ordering. Guides come without binders unless specified.

Users Guides

CompuServe Information Service Users Guide, spiral bound for easy reading $10.95

Service-Specific Users Guides

Advanced CompuServe for IBM power users $19.95
How To Get the Most Out Of CompuServe $19.95
IQINT — CompuServe's Company Reported Financial Data Interface
 for Microcomputer Financial Software — Users Guide $4.95
Let's Talk: An Introduction To CompuServe's Citizen's Band Simulator $4.95
Mini-Guide To Online Computing $2.95
MQINT — CompuServe's Financial Market Data Interface
 for Microcomputer Financial Software — Users Guide $4.95
Personal File Area Users Guide $10.95

Game Guides

Guide To CompuServe Games $17.45
MegaWars I Users Guide $7.95
MegaWars III Users Guide $6.95
Island of Kesmai Users Guide $19.00
MegaWars I Users Guide plus blueprint series $13.95
MegaWars I package $16.95

File-Generating & Text-Editing Guides

EDIT (FILGE) Users Guide $4.49

Binders

CompuServe logo vinyl binder with 1″ spine for 8 1/2″ x 11″ pages $3.95
CompuServe logo vinyl binder with 1 1/2″ spine for 8 1/2″ x 11″ pages $2.95

CompuServe Communications Software

The Professional Connection for the IBM PC, XT and PCjr (on 5 1/4″ diskettes) with binder $49.95
CompuServe VIDTEX for Apple II (on 5 1/4″ diskette) with binder $39.95
CompuServe VIDTEX for Atari 800, 800 XL, 600 XL with 64 K, 1200 XL, 65 XE, 130 XE $39.95
CompuServe VIDTEX for Commodore 64 (two versions: cassette tape or 5 1/4″ diskette) with binder $39.95
CompuServe VIDTEX for TRS-80 Model II, TRSDOS required (on 5 1/4″ diskette) with binder $39.95
CompuServe VIDTEX for TRS-80 Model III, TRSDOS required (on 5 1/4″ diskette) with binder $39.95
CompuServe VIDTEX for TRS-80 Color Computer
 (two versions: on cassette tape or 5 1/4″ diskette) with binder $39.95

Personal Color Radar Software

For the IBM PC with 128K RAM (on 5 1/4″ diskette) with binder $59.95
For the TRS-80 Color Computer with 32K RAM Computer (on 5 1/4″ diskette) with binder $59.95

PERSONAL EASYPLEX DIRECTORY

Name _____ CompuServe User ID Number _____

Address _____

City/State/Zip _____ Phone Number _____

Name _____ CompuServe User ID Number _____

Address _____

City/State/Zip _____ Phone Number _____

Name _____ CompuServe User ID Number _____

Address _____

City/State/Zip _____ Phone Number _____

Name _____ CompuServe User ID Number _____

Address _____

City/State/Zip _____ Phone Number _____

Name _____ CompuServe User ID Number _____

Address _____

City/State/Zip _____ Phone Number _____

Name _____ CompuServe User ID Number _____

Address _____

City/State/Zip _____ Phone Number _____

PERSONAL EASYPLEX DIRECTORY

Name _____   CompuServe User ID Number _____

Address _____

City/State/Zip _____   Phone Number _____

Name _____   CompuServe User ID Number _____

Address _____

City/State/Zip _____   Phone Number _____

Name _____   CompuServe User ID Number _____

Address _____

City/State/Zip _____   Phone Number _____

Name _____   CompuServe User ID Number _____

Address _____

City/State/Zip _____   Phone Number _____

Name _____   CompuServe User ID Number _____

Address _____

City/State/Zip _____   Phone Number _____

Name _____   CompuServe User ID Number _____

Address _____

City/State/Zip _____   Phone Number _____

PERSONAL EASYPLEX DIRECTORY

Name _____ CompuServe User ID Number _____

Address _____

City/State/Zip _____ Phone Number _____

Name _____ CompuServe User ID Number _____

Address _____

City/State/Zip _____ Phone Number _____

Name _____ CompuServe User ID Number _____

Address _____

City/State/Zip _____ Phone Number _____

Name _____ CompuServe User ID Number _____

Address _____

City/State/Zip _____ Phone Number _____

Name _____ CompuServe User ID Number _____

Address _____

City/State/Zip _____ Phone Number _____

Name _____ CompuServe User ID Number _____

Address _____

City/State/Zip _____ Phone Number _____

PERSONAL EASYPLEX DIRECTORY

Name   CompuServe User ID Number

Address

City/State/Zip   Phone Number

Name   CompuServe User ID Number

Address

City/State/Zip   Phone Number

Name   CompuServe User ID Number

Address

City/State/Zip   Phone Number

Name   CompuServe User ID Number

Address

City/State/Zip   Phone Number

Name   CompuServe User ID Number

Address

City/State/Zip   Phone Number

Name   CompuServe User ID Number

Address

City/State/Zip   Phone Number

PERSONAL EASYPLEX DIRECTORY

_____
Name

_____
Address

_____
City/State/Zip

_____
CompuServe User ID Number

_____
Phone Number

_____
Name

_____
Address

_____
City/State/Zip

_____
CompuServe User ID Number

_____
Phone Number

_____
Name

_____
Address

_____
City/State/Zip

_____
CompuServe User ID Number

_____
Phone Number

_____
Name

_____
Address

_____
City/State/Zip

_____
CompuServe User ID Number

_____
Phone Number

_____
Name

_____
Address

_____
City/State/Zip

_____
CompuServe User ID Number

_____
Phone Number

_____
Name

_____
Address

_____
City/State/Zip

_____
CompuServe User ID Number

_____
Phone Number

INDEX

INDEX

INDEX